Myth, Magic, and Metaphor

Metaphor

A Journey into the Heart of Creativity

Myth, Magic, and Metaphor

and

Metaphor

A Journey into the Heart of Creativity

Patricia Daly-Lipe

JADA

Myth, Magic, and Metaphor
All Rights Reserved, 2005, by Patricia Daly-Lipe, Ph.D.

Cover painting by Patricia Daly-Lipe, Ph.D.
Nude Descending a Staircase Marcel Duchamp, page 98
© 2005 Artists Rights Society (ARS), New York / ADAGP, Paris / Succession Marcel Duchamp

Published in 2005 by JADA Press
Jacksonville, Florida
www.JadaPress.com
Third Edition

ISBN: 097641-158X LCCN: 2005928396

First Edition - Published 1999 by 1st Books Library
ISBN - 0-97449-385-6   LCCN: 2003112753
Second Edition - Published 2001 by 1st Books Library
ISBN: 1-58500-337-9

Printed in the United States of America

About the Book

Myth, Magic, & Metaphor, attempts to put together a fairly simple creative writing classroom scenario. The idea is to awaken the aesthetic sense, the creative muse who lurks within us all. The method is multisensory, interdisciplinary, and holistic. Philosophy, art, music, and linguistics are some of the disciplines used. The goal is to have the reader recognize and enjoy the process. It asks for the students of writing to experience the sense of wonder they knew as children, to use their imagination, to feel and absorb the world around them, to listen, not just to hear, to see, not just to look, in sum, to become intoxicated with life. The tool is the heart: the medium is words.

"They say that the human mind, once stretched to a new idea, never returns to its original shape." (Georgi Lozanov). Our hope is that this little tome will reshape a few minds.

Nature Quote

"Love of Nature, that strong feeling of enthusiasm which leads to a profound admiration of the whole works of creation, belongs, it may be presumed, to a certain peculiarity of organization, and has, no doubt, existed in different individuals from the beginning of the world. The old poets and philosophers, romance-writers and troubadours, had all looked upon Nature with observing and admiring eyes. They have most of them given incidentally charming pictures of Spring, of the setting sun, of peculiar spots, and of favorite flowers.

"There are few writers of note, of any country or of any age, from whom quotations might not be made in proof of the love with which they regarded Nature."

Paul and Virginia by Bernardin de Saint-Pierre
From the early 1900's (No date of publication)

Acknowledgements

This book owes its existence to my students. I do not believe we can learn to write. We do, however, learn when we write. In the same vein, I did not teach my students. I provided a blueprint, an impetus, an environment for them to achieve their goal. But it was their interest and enthusiasm that also taught and inspired me.

A thank you is also given to all the readers who have, since the book's first publication in 1999, written to offer their appreciation and gratitude as well as to the pople who have asked me to give talks about our theme, creativity.

I am also indebted to and appreciative of the patience, encouragement and left-brained, fact finding skill of my dear husband, Steele Lipe.

Table of Contents

Finding The Writer Within 11

Introduction 13

1. Words 17

2. There Are No Rules 33

3. Back To Words 41

4. Music 55

5. Imagination 67

6. The Mystery 75

7. More Music 83

8. Analogy of Painting 89

9. Participation 103

10. Symbols, Math and Nature 109

11. The Metaphor 129

12. Myth 137

13. The Process 145

14. Reading and Writing, it's Therapy! 149

15. Summary 157

Finding The Writer Within

A Journey Into The Heart of Creativity

We do not write in order to be understood; we write in order to understand.

(C. Day Lewis)

[It is] out of what I don't know that I begin to write.
(Toni Morrison)

We need more poetry that reveals what the heart is ready to recognize.

(Joseph Campbell)

Make connections...always make connections... (and always be prepared for) unscheduled flights of fancy.

(Lucia St. Clair Robson)

Nobody can advise and help you, nobody. There is only one single means. Go inside yourself. Discover the motive that bids you [to] write; examine whether it sends its roots down to the deepest places of your heart.

(Rainer Maria Rilke)

Introduction

In post 9/11 and all the wars and battles we have experienced since then, let us not loose sight of one fact. We are all, despite race, creed, tradition, or location, human. And as human beings, we share this planet, a small ball spinning around within a gigantic universe (which may be but one of many universes). The scope of our environment, going to the stars and beyond, is immeasurable and yet, within each one of us lurks a bright light waiting to be released. The light has no limits. It has no structure. It is called creativity.

I call creativity the muse who lies in wait within us all. She wants us to recognize her, to free her so she might express herself. She is a gift that binds us as mortals to something much bigger. Organization, rules, limits of all sorts are taking over our psyches and the idea of no rules and the ambiguity of intuition are frightening concepts to so many of us today. But there is new word that is catching on and communicating to us on many levels. The word is 'globalization' and it implies extensive opportunities for truly worldwide development. Globalization is the result of a historical process and it reflects both human innovations and technological progress. But the good news is that globalization also begs for creativity. There is dynamism to creativity; an enthusiasm that is generated deep within the individual. Creativity empowers a release of tension. For this reason alone, it is essential.

This book was originally written with the encouragement of Richard Lederer in 1999. So much has changed since then. In this little tome, I encourage an interdisciplinary approach to weed out the creative muse. The readers' recognition of their own creativity can be expressed in many disciplines from the creative arts to science, but my main focus is writing. Each of us has a story. We relate to the world in as many billions of ways as there are humans on the planet. Whether you are a scientist, a technician, a doctor, a housewife or an artist, you have something unique to say. So let the words flow. Allow them to topple, trip, and stumble. Play. Enjoy. Explore. Dr. Seuss (Theodor Seuss Geisel in real life) said, "Adults are obsolete children." Let the child come out; he is in there just waiting to be released again. As a child, remember how you tumbled through life. No condemning. No judgments. Free.

Try out the words and let them try out you. The words are not demons. Let them—and believe me, they will—take over. Sit back, laugh, cry as the words flow. Watch as the imaginary becomes the actual. Experience the mystery, the magic of seeing, written on a page, words that you never could have imagined writing. Talk about therapy! Vincent Scully, the great Yale architectural historian said it best. "Put the right words together with the visual facts so that all of a sudden sparks fly and a new skill is born—the ability to see."

The key to writing is writing. Phyllis Whitney said, "I think with a pencil." For you it may be a keyboard. But your real tool is your mind. Your medium is words.

Hélène Cixous, Professor at the University of Paris VIII and a remarkable author, wrote in *Coming To Writing*:

"In the beginning, I adored. What I adored was human. Not persons; not totalities, not defined and named beings. But signs. Flashes of being that glanced off me, kindling me. Lightening-like bursts that came to me: Look! I blazed up. And the sign withdrew. Vanished. While I burned on and consumed myself wholly. What had reached me, so powerfully cast from a human body, was Beauty…. A desire was seeking its home. I was that desire. I was the question. The question with this strange destiny; to seek, to pursue the answers that will appease it…."

Problematically, in that unsettled, indefinable way that the creative muse works, Mlle Cixous concedes (with a chuckle, I assume), "Yet what misfortune if the question should happen to meet its answer!"

It is, after all, the journey not the destination that brings its rewards. Writing opens doors, doors which lead not to answers but to more questions. Writing is a way of introducing wonder and surprise to ourselves. To use Mlle Cixous' words, "My writing watches. Eyes closed."

That mysterious faculty, which some call genius, cannot be 'taught'. But it can be discovered.

Look for the extra-ordinary in the ordinary. Go a step further and take the 'order' out of 'ordinary'. For example, you might remember some incident or thing which may have seemed commonplace at the time but which, upon reflection, you found significant. Write about the incident and as you write, let the words take control. You may find that the words move up from a simple description to a plateau of revelation. Writing does that. It is a combination of intuition, desire, and open-mindedness combined with hard work, long hours, and a solid foundation that allow a writer to write and to write creatively. In the pages that follow, it is hoped that this small tome will assist you, the reader, to become the writer and discover your own creative muse.

1

Words

"In the beginning was the Word; and the Word was with God; and the Word was God."

(The Gospel According to John)

"The word is a sign or symbol of the impressions or affections of the soul."

(Aristotle)

L anguage contains everything from history, to sociology, economics, philosophy, religious thought, even stories. Think of the word 'community' as meaning 'common unity'. Language has been used and abused throughout history but it still reflects human destiny and reveals all that is known of life itself.

Language is ACTIVE; language USES us!

"The genius of democracies," wrote Alex de Toqueville in 1840, "is seen not only in the great number of new words introduced but even more in the new ideas they express." To which, in 1936, Willa Cather might be said to reply, "Give the people a new word and they think they have a new fact." Let's look at words.

According to Webster's Dictionary, 'to think' means "to have the mind occupied on some subject; to judge, to intend, to imagine, to consider." It is a transitive verb which means that thinking requires an object. As Paul Brunton stated in *The Hidden Teaching Beyond Yoga*, "…we cannot see any object without *thinking* of it as being seen. If it is to exist for us at all, it must exist as something that is perceived." And he takes his case a step further. "We perceive the object because we think it; we do not think the object because we perceive it." First the thought, then the thing. (For an in-depth and fascinating discussion of language and the origin of language verses thought, read *Thought and Language* by Lev Vygotsky in the 'newly revised' edition by Alex Kozulin.) The conclusion of this mini-debate is this. My very existence (as a member of the human race) is defined by thought and whether thought or the object perceived comes first is for you to decide. Nevertheless, whichever use you utilize, the connection between thought and perception is directly related to mankind's very nature which is social. We co-exist on this planet, for better or worse and we communicate with words.

> "Man's mind enables him to form concepts, use language, build societies and cultures; above all, it enables him to work in intellectual community (where)…the emotional and intellectual life of each man is sustained by his unity with others."
> (J. Bronowski's review of Teilhard de Chardin's *The Future of Man*)

Life is a journey. The base of the word 'journey', is 'jour' meaning day (from the French). Language reveals the journey, the daily experiences which are life. To be more precise, language reveals our own or some other person's observation. The testimony of the senses leads us to accept multiplicity and change; every moment we see or observe a new image or mental observation of what we call life. A smell, a sound, a touch, each sense stimulates an entire storehouse of memory. These moments are what Friedrich Nietzsche called the "creative truths". However, language is more than name-calling. Toni Morrison said in her acceptance speech for the Nobel Prize for Literature in 1993, "The vitality of language lies in its ability to limn the actual, imaged, and possible lives of its speakers, readers, and writers.... It arcs toward the place where meaning may lie." We will explore what the "meaning" or the "creative truths" are as the chapters progress, but let it be established here that history is not defined by dates and names. History is someone's point of view, someone's experience in a particular time in the development (or decay) of the human race. It can be said that historical fiction is a combination of two nouns. The fiction being what is inside your or the protagonist's mind at the time of an event and history the time and event. Since history is recorded by people, and since all people are prone to their own perspective on what they see, then it might be said that all history is fiction.

"Novels arise out of the shortcomings of history."

(F. von Hardenberg,
Later Novalis, Fragmente und Studien, 1799 - 1800)

Let us return to another history, the history of words. Open a dictionary and explore. Mark Twain joked, "I have studied [a dictionary] often, but I never could discover the plot." Every word in the dictionary, however, has a plot of its own, its etymology. We understand that individual words, especially nouns, contain history, sociology, economics, politics, and/or drama, keeping in mind that they change and evolve with each generation and sometimes come and go and return in a new context. It can be like a complex maze to attempt to follow the historical trail of a word. But let us begin anyway and choose a word that depicts the essence of what is called 'life'. It is a word which is not static. Instead it reflects the flow which is life. The word is inspiration.

"Inspiration is more important than knowledge."

(Albert Einstein)

"Inspiration may be a form of superconsciousness, or perhaps of subconsciousness—I wouldn't know. But I am sure it is the antithesis of self-conscious."

(Aaron Copeland)

Inspiration, as we shall see as the chapters progress can be said to be the alluring voice of creativity. Inspiration is also the genesis of the word 'creativity'.

> "Be but thy inspiration given,
> No matter though what danger sought,
> I'll fathom hell or climb to heaven,
> And yet esteem that cheap which love has
>   bought.
> Fame cannot tempt the bard
> Who's famous with his God,
> Nor laurel him reward
> Who has his maker's nod."
>
> (Henry David Thoreau,
> *Inspiration,* last two stanzas)

The etymology of inspiration is the Latin word, *inspiratus*, past participle of *inspirare* meaning to blow or breathe upon. Thus, if we follow the evolutionary/etymological sequence through, creativity refers to the life-giving force: breath. When a baby comes out of the womb, he breathes for the first time on his own and begins life as we know it. Analogous to this birthing is the creative process represented by the writer, the painter, the musician or the dancer. Isadora Duncan, the great innovative interpreter of dance at the turn of the twentieth century, spoke of the "state of complete suspense" which proceeds the so-called spontaneous creative activity (dance or music or painting or writing). This non-verbal excitement, dreamlike, vague, ambiguous comes *before* the creative act or action. Stephen Spender, English poet and critic, expressed this time as "a dim cloud of an idea which I feel must be condensed into a shower of words."

> "All writing requires at least some measure of trance-like state: the writer must summon out of nonexistence some character, some scene, and he must focus that imaginary scene in his mind until he sees it vividly as, in another state, he would see the typewriter or cluttered desk in front of him.... But at times...something happens. A demon takes over...and the imagery becomes real."
>
> (John Gardner)

Be beguiled by your own unconscious mind. Allow the door to your unconscious to open, then watch what flows out on the paper before you and read the words in awe.

> "It is our idleness,
> in our dreams,
> that the submerged
> truth sometimes
> comes to the top."
>
> (Virginia Woolf)

Take the word 'idleness' and respect it. Idleness does not connote laziness. It is our time to be silent and one with the world around us. The silence is golden when absorbed. "A man should learn to detect and watch that gleam of light which flashes across his mind from within, more than the lustre of the firmament of bards and sages." (Ralph Waldo Emerson, *Self-Reliance*) What you did not know that you knew will suddenly come forth and you will begin to write and to write well. "A man never rises so high as when he knows not whither he is going." (Oliver Cromwell) Isabel Illende, when she wrote the poignant novel/diary, *Paula*, to her daughter, (also named Paula) explaining herself, her past, her present, and her life as a writer, counseled that the writer must "believe the unbelievable."

Once again, to quote the first great philospher born on American soil, Ralph Waldo Emerson, "We but half express ourselves, and are ashamed of that divine idea which each of us represents." First, believe in yourself. Second, make connections; always make connections. Be aware of what you see, what you feel, what you smell. Sink into the scene. Be ready for and allow "unscheduled flights of fancy!" (Lucia St. Clair Robson, author)

> "God guard me from those thoughts men think
> In the mind alone,
> He that sings a lasting song
> Thinks in a marrow bone...
> I pray—for fashion's word is out

And Prayer comes round again—
That I may seem though I die old
A foolish, passionate man."

(William Butler Yeats)

To create is to give birth, the act of bringing forth something new. First and foremost, the artist/author/musician/dancer is a human being. As such he or she is both created and a creator. As a creator, a person gives birth to something that the rational and language-imbued world has never known before.

As far as we know, the human is the only being who is conscious of being conscious. Not satisfied with just accepting what happens to us, we, as human beings, naturally inspect and challenge every move, every thought. Philosophers from Heraclitus to Plato, from the Buddha to Nietzsche have catechized and questioned the creative process. Friedrich Nietzsche, in *Composition on Thus Spoke Zarathustra*, wrote about the notion of revelation or the creation of a new idea. A new idea, he said, is something "profoundly convulsive and disturbing" which "suddenly becomes visible and audible with indescribable definiteness and exactness…a thought flashes out like lightning, inevitably without hesitation—I have never had any choice about it."

According to the Buddha, "…as the mind returns to its natural state of integrity and non-duality, it ceases to clutch at experience with the symbols of discursive thought. It simply perceives without words or concepts." (A note should be made here about the Buddha. To quote Joseph Campbell, "the reference to the life of the Buddha is quite secondary. The accent in Hinduism and Buddhism is the relevance of the symbolic forms to your own life. You understand these things inward to yourself.") Following the Buddhist concept, you could say that the 'truth' comes like lightening as a flash of understanding (to paraphrase Neitzsche). It is outside of time and space. It is beyond words. Once the mind has perceived this 'truth' (Nirvana), it reverts back to reality (as we know it) and to discourse and the written word. James Joyce spoke of an "aesthetic arrest" or "stasis". It is that point where you are aware of the silence within the very center of activity in the world and of the universe. It is there, he says (marrying the East with the West in thought) that "the mind is arrested and raised above desire and loathing" and "the world is recognized as a revelation sufficient in itself." For Joyce, even (and most often) the most trivial things could be invested with "epiphanies". In *Portrait Of An Artist As A Young Man*, the protagonist Stephen Dedalus says, the 'soul' or 'whatness' of an object or a gesture or a phrase "leaps to us from the vestment of its appearance."

Plato, probably one of the greatest of all Western philosophers, 470–399 BC, using the voice of Socrates (who, like the Buddha, never wrote anything down and could represent more than one philosopher or thinker), stated that for art (by this we encompass any of the art forms including creative writing) to be truly noble, it must reveal "something of that essence which is eternal...."

Whether understood from an Eastern perspective or a Western conviction/belief/philosophy, it must be concluded that there is something very mysterious about the concept and the process of creativity. Isn't it exciting to think that you, the writer, are actively involved in this, the very essence of life itself? To quote Nietzsche again, "For art to exist, or any sort of aesthetic activity or perception to exist, a certain psychological precondition is indispensable: *intoxication*." (The italic emphasis is my enthusiasm being expressed visually. The etymology of 'enthusiasm', is, by the way, 'in or of God'. So you see how individual words can speak volumes.)

The word 'creativity' seems to be an anachronism to the modern era of high technology with its computer networks, fiberoptics, complex and intrinsically specialized data bases, all of which require logical thought processes, a definite rationale, facts, and information. In this environment, it is difficult to justify, much less explain, the need, actually the necessity, to take time out, to 'listen' to the silence, to gaze in wonderment at a leaf or a flicker of light, to be quiet enough to be startled. Fear of sponteneity, nonconformity, irrationality, and the unconscious and subconscious mind has been encouraged by the gurus of computer literacy. Even they had, at one time, to wean themselves from the so-called mystical traditions, be they religious, philosophical, or even folklore.

Tom Robbins cautions, "...the mission of the artist in an overtechnologized society [is] to call the old magic back to life." We will talk about magic later; just keep it in the back of your mind for now.

> "Tools and techniques ought to be an extension of consciousness, but they can just as easily be a protection from consciousness. Then the tools become defense mechanisms...specifically against the wider and more complex dimensions of consciousness that we call the unconscious."
>
> (Rollo May, *The Courage to Create*)

Why are so many people frightened to not have the answers? Is the world so scary, so demanding, that we cannot take time out, ask the questions and even admit we simply do not know the answers? Inspiration comes from the roaming of free imagination, but it takes time.

I am writing on my PC computer which has Windows XP and Word 2003, plus many other exciting accessories. I have come to depend on this machine completely for everything from writing to reference, from fax to internet access. Last year, it was attacked by a virus (personification in the computer world!). With sheer terror, I ran to my technical guru. "Save my novel," I cried, loosing all sense of decorum and composure. Fortunately he did, but it was at great expense. I lost both time and money. Nevertheless, to benefit from the experience, I translated it as a sign/warning/omen. The real source of creativity was not my computer but ME! Some sick individual was taking great pleasure in sucking out my words one line at a time (the virus even made a sucking sound: "slop, slop, slop") and the hacker didn't even know me! My pleasure had been the process of writing. What was his (or possibly, hers)?

Benjamin Lee Whorf, an American linguistic scientist in the early nineteen hundreds, believed that there was no primitive language per se. Contrary to his contemporaries like Rudolf Steiner, Sigmund Freud, and Carl Jung, Whorf maintained that the structure of language one uses directly influences the way one thinks. "[T]he content of thought influences the process of thought…so that generalization about process becomes impossible without its content being taken into account." Language, according to Whorf, is a "classification and arrangement of the stream of sensory experience which results in a certain world-order, a certain segment of the world that is easily expressible by the type of symbolic means that language employs." By Whorf's definition, there is no room for the non-verbal, dreamlike, spontaneous urge. Clearly his logic is appealing; but that is what it is, rational and logical. The computer acts the same rational way. It is programmed based on logic. However, spontaneity, the creative urge, something 'new' depicted by the artistic mind does not come from the machine or from logical deductions. Nor is creativity confined to the artist; it is also essential to the scientist and to scientific inquiry. "[N]ature is not perfectly rational and does not efficiently fulfill her own longing for perfection." (Friedrich Nietzsche) The scientist, if he is going to discover something absolutely new, must be open to the concepts of inspiration, imagination, and creativity.

We have come a long way from the initial search into the source of creativity and even further from the search into the meaning and use of our medium; words. However, I hope my reader will consider the various arguments and opinions and continue to accept little and question all and everything. It is a healthy exercise and, at the very least, will prevent atrophy of the brain.

> "As a human being (the artist) may have many moods and a will and personal aims, but as an artist he is 'man' in a higher sense—he is 'collective man'—one who carries and shapes the unconscious, psychic life of mankind."
>
> (Carl Jung)

André Bréton, author of the *Surrealist Manifesto* (first edition, 1924), felt (perhaps thanks to Sigmund Freud) that "the imagination is…on the point of reclaiming its right." Surrealism called up the irrational world of the subconscious to reveal itself through the medium of an art form, be it painting, music, dance or writing. Way back in the fifteenth century, Leonardo da Vinci had already suggested "the possibility of self-revelation through automatic writing." (Paul J. Sachs, *Modern Paintings and Drawings*) A more recent artist, Salvador Dali, is quoted as saying once, "I am the first to be surprised and often terrified by the images that I see appear on my canvas."

Untitled (c. 1925)   Daly Highleyman

I wonder as new faces meet
That smile, then pass me by
I wonder at all life around
The stars, the moon, the sky.

And yet at times I wonder—what
Just wonder what is meant
By wonders that I've wondered
In times long past and spend.

                                        Daly Highleyman

I do believe that deep down within our very being is the source of creativity and it is that very source which connects to the primal rhythms of the universe. There is no clear boundary between ourselves and the world which we observe. Watching the brilliant orange rays descend into a soft rosy glow at sunset; looking at bare, snow-covered limbs of a tree angling upward toward the sky; peering through the newly opened petals of a rose; all these pictures capture our imagination. The observer "plays a creative role in the observation." (Robert Hand) So do not think you must have something to say before you put words on paper. Let the insights, visions, ideas happen in the process of writing.

> "Writing is a process in which we discover what lives in us. The writing reveals what is alive.... The deepest satisfaction of writing is precisely that it opens up new spaces within each of us of which we were not aware before we started to write."
>
> (Nouwen, *Reflections*)

Look at the picture on the following page. Another probably drawn in the 1920s by my father, Daly Highleyman, this drawing obviously opened up some "new spaces" for him!

Untitled, c. 1920s   Daly Highleyman

Write keeping this Indian adage in mind, "All this struggling to learn, when all we have to do is remember."

2

There Are No Rules

"…[B]ut, of course, art didn't have laws….
That was what made art better than life. Or,
if not superior, at least more interesting."
(Tom Robbins, *skinny legs and all*)

One of the first things I tell my class of potential novelists and poets is, "There are no rules." Writing comes from the heart. The creative muse lurks within us one and all. Antoine de St. Exupery, pilot and author of *The Little Prince*, wrote, "And now here is my secret, a very simple secret; it is only with the heart that one can see rightly; what is essential is invisible to the eye." And, in the Bible, Moses told the Isrealites that God sent them into the wilderness to "learn what is in your heart." What is wonderful and exciting about writing is that something which is invisible to the eye expresses itself. What you did not know you knew comes out as the words spill across the page. It is a cleansing and it is a self-enriching experience. No one else can do it for you. You are unique. Love yourself; love your uniqueness; and get to know the real 'you' as the words flow.

While many striving authors attempt to tap into something called 'creativity', searching for some 'force' (reminiscent of *Star Wars*) to spur them on to success, spilling out unique verbage and insight, I am inclined to believe that they would do well to step back and read the classics. Begin at the beginning: the *Bible*. According to this great book, God created man in His own image. Think about that. What is it about humanity that separates man from other animals? What is it about each individual that makes him or her unique? Sometimes it takes a confrontation with death or squalor, war or disease, for man to appreciate and recognize (re-know) the essence, the spirit, the soul within. The body decays; the soul persists. Read William James' work for his study of human nature and the varieties of religious experience. Once it has perceived 'the truth', the mind reverts to discourse and the written word. In the 2004 Mythic Journeys Conference in Atlanta honoring Joseph Campbell, both Robert Bly and Michael Meade made impassioned pleas for participants to honor Campbell not just by reading his works, but by "doing as he did—tell stories!" And it is true; the only way to give birth to a truth or vision is to take it inside yourself, make it your own, and then give it back to the world, refreshed by its incubation in your soul. This is where myths are born...but more about myths later.

Let us approach this topic from another vantage point. It was interesting for me to find, while doing research on another project, that many of the world's scientists and mathematicians were also astrologers. Astrology has been used by many to explain man's place in the universe, in the scheme of things (should there exist an underlying 'scheme'). I found an old book in my father's library called *A Manual of Cheirosophy*. It was written in 1885. In the preface, the author, E. D. Heron-Allen, states, "...my aim in writing this *Manual of Cheirosophy* having been simply to place before the world a concise and clearly comprehensible epitome of the principia of a science which opens a page of the great book of nature to the student who will diligently read it...and which endows all men who will study it with the foresight which, under the name of intuitive faculty, is the cherished possession of so few, enunciating and solving the great problem of 'Know Thyself'." Cheirosophy, I found out, is a means by which the past, the present, and the future can be read "in the formation of the hand". It is, evidently, more than mere palmistry. The point here, however, is that every successive generation has sought a way to fathom the mysteries of the universe outside of 'pure' science. Einstein himself pointed out that the "most beautiful experience we can have is the mysterious. It is," he said, "the fundamental emotion which stands at the cradle of true art and true science." And, he admonishes, "[w]hoever does not know it and can no longer wonder, no longer marvel, is as good as dead, and his eyes are dimmed." Marvel, wonder, delight, these are the words shared by the great men of science as well as history and art in man's eternal quest for the meaning of the mysteries, of life itself

"Until we accept the fact that life itself is founded in mystery, we shall learn nothing."

(Henry Miller)

Spiritualists believe that we only use a fraction of what our minds are capable of. They believe people create veils (the etymology of reveal being 'remove the veil') that prevent them from seeing clearly. It is necessary for us all to recognize the veils' existence and to consciously attempt to remove them, to take away the rules and regulations that blur our vision of truths and allow our inner voice, our creative muse to speak.

Consider keeping a diary. "A diarist is a writer who watches himself watching himself." (Edward Robb Ellis) Write about what you can see and what you cannot 'see'. Have you ever experienced the 'crucible effect'? Crises are change-points. Crises show us who we really are. Divorce, bereavement, disease, war, persecution, loss of a job, all force us to realize what is vital in life and what is peripheral. Anger is toxic. Unexpressed, it will erode your inner peace. The pages of a diary provide a safe place to explore anxious or painful feelings. Empty out the pockets of your life in a diary.

"We are here to abet Creation and to witness it, to notice each thing so that each thing gets noticed. Together we notice not only each mountain shadow and each stone

on the beach but we notice each other's beautiful faces and complex natures so that Creation need not play to an empty house."
(Annie Dillard in a statement on 'The Meaning of Life' for *Life Magazine*)

For wonderful examples of diary or memoir writing, I recommend Persig's, *Zen and the Art of Motorcycle Maintenance* and Frank McCourt's poignant *Angela's Ashes* (winner of the Pulitzer Prize). A little history: diarists were prolific in the nineteenth century. A diary was the equivalent of a Confessional. Also in the 19th century, correspondence letters were most revealing. Letters were written on a daily basis, sometimes just to ask if an individual could visit a neighbor at a certain hour, (preferably in the daylight hours according to the rules of proper etiquette). There were no telephones and it would be most improper to just show up at the doorstep. Then there were newspapers to consider as a kind of memoir. Meetings of neighbors and meals served at receptions in private homes were just as important as world events in the nineteenth and early twentieth century. News and correspondence took time in those days. It took, for example, five weeks before the British heard that their troops had successfully burned the nation's Capital and the President's Mansion (as the White House was called before it was rebuilt and painted after the fire). The year was 1814. The news was delivered and digested by the British, but while the English were congratulating themselves, the Americans had already commenced reconstruction. The facts were correct but the emotions reigned and the plan was ultimately defeated. Washington remained the Capital of the new nation. Not content with facts, authors do not simply find out the when and where, but they evaluate what they find. And since each one of us is different, our perspective is different. The writer of memoirs writes what he or she felt when the event happened which may or may not go along with the facts. However, these feelings paint a more powerful picture of the occurrence than mere facts.

Today, we still have a need to write, but as Anthony Pitch, historian and author of several books on the history of Washington, D.C., today's private thoughts are written on "paper purchased at Staples around the corner from Starbucks." So much is lost as emails are obliterated by a click of the mouse. Nevertheless, the need to write survives. It is part of human nature.

John Livingston Lowes (1867-1945) author of *The Road to Zanadu*, said he wrote the book because it "simply came" as "the imaginative energy itself" surprised and forced him to write. This wonderful book tells the story of the genesis of *The Rime of the Ancient Mariner* and *Kubla Khan*. Published in 1927, the book literally dazzled the public. Beyond being simply a stale, scholarly guide to the two Coleridge poems ("two of the greatest poems of our language", according to the *Yale Review*), it was "a landmark and a guide post in literary scholarship"

(*The Saturday Review of Literature*) and "a biggish, jolly book, whose effortless ease conceals the years of toil that went to its making, and pleasant reading from end to end." (John Bakeless, author and editor) In a period of American history when Germany was the center of intellectual endeavor and culture, it was exciting to have an American inspired to write such a tome. But for the author, it was "an adventure like a passage, through the mazes of a labyrinth, to come out at last upon a wide and open sky." Professor Lowes said that *The Road to Zanadu* was but a symbol of something intangible. It was research into the energy of the imagination itself. "We sometimes forget creative energy creates," he warns us. Take a word. Mix it with thought. Out of the mix comes something new and unique. "The ways of creation are wrapped in mystery; we may only marvel and bow the head."

Your assignment is to slow down. Take time out. Do not just 'hear', listen; do not just 'see', look.

3

Back to Words

"…[T]he artist, like the God of creation, remains within or behind or beyond or above his handiwork, invisible, refined out of existence, indifferent…."

(James Joyce)

Words come to us from many places. They come with a history, with a story. This is sometimes their etymology. It can also come from their actual use at a given place in a given time by a given person. Some words come alone but most come in company with other words. As to the latter, I cannot stress too much the importance of grammar. English does not, like so many other languages, add endings to words to explain a word's use in the sentence. Rather, its position within the sentence dictates the word's significance. It is essential to know syntax, that is, the arrangement of words in a sentence and to recognize the proper positioning of words (with the appropriate punctuation) and reproduce the same in your own writing. A delightful example of misplaced positioning is the following:

Mrs. Smith was awarded a bronze plaque as Jefferson County Mother of the Year for having born ten children by Judge Jones in ceremonies at the community center yesterday.

Another one:

Mouth to mouth artificial respiration can be used on anyone who has swallowed something that will block his breathing, especially a small child.

If you would like some homework, try punctuating the following paragraph:

At the banquet will be many members of Congress eating roast beef and members of the press as well. The waiters will serve the courses of soup fish salad meat and vegetables and dessert with three wines. For dessert women tend to prefer sherbet men pie and ice cream. Mind your manners and try not to eat too much. Please try not to drop your spoon or roll in your soup. Stay awake during the after-dinner speech and if you must yawn do so quietly.

We have had many laughs over that one!

When used effectively, grammar can contribute not only to the atmosphere and mood of a literary work but to its power and significance as well.

In class, we spoke of words coming to us from many places. The United States is a melting pot and all the more rich because of it. New words are introduced each year as people from all over the world come to live in America and share their heritage. New dictionaries are being published constantly to keep up with the growth of the English/American language. Today at the dawn of the twenty-first century, American English has become the second largest language in the world and the secondary language of most of the world's population. For writers, this language with its annual growth in vocabulary provides a rich reservoir of words and with each new word comes a taste of history and tradition from other cultures as well as added nuance.

The structure of the language that is habitually spoken strongly influences the manner in which a person understands the environment in which he or she lives. Consider some languages in which there are no adjectives or the languages in which there are no verbs. Certainly people speaking those languages have a different view of the universe. If the content of thought influences the process of thought and the content is contingent upon language, then just consider how amazing it is that we, on this small planet with the many varieties of linguistic patterns, can even begin to understand one another. Even within the United States the language structure changes among ethnic groups and from one geographic area to another.

Common idiomatic usage is defined as slang. Someone has called slang 'a kind of linguistic exuberance.' Related to standard vocabulary slang could be equated to dancing as it relates to music. Chesterton is quoted as saying, "All slang is metaphor, and all metaphor is poetry." (from *Words on Words, A Dictionary for Writers and Others Who Care About Words*, John B. Bremner)

Think of all the synonyms there are today for the word 'relax': ease up, mellow out, chill, take it easy, be cool, kick back. Since relaxation is supposed to be the first step toward wisdom, intuition, and creativity, I cannot help but wonder what saying 'chill' would do toward helping a person prepare for "higher thoughts". But the real problem with slang is its short life. For the writer to emphasize a particular time/place/person/culture, however, it is hard to beat the lingo.

I cannot emphasize too much the significance of the word both as a symbol and an image. This symbol or image is representative of itself and more than itself. How is this achieved? What is the desired result? Why? Before we progress to the creative aspect of words, we need to lay a good, solid foundation. Just as a building does not begin with a roof, a story does not begin without structure and background.

The background begins with the history of words, their derivation, their origin, in other words their etymology. Etymology adds to our depth and understanding of words. As we stated before, the English language is rich in its heritage: Latin, Greek, Scandinavian, Old French, German, and more. Knowing the etymology of a word is like giving it a halo. The light (or aura) from the halo takes in the enclosure or surroundings of the word. I am attempting to portray, figuratively, the word's connotation. Unlike its connotation, a word's denotation is its definition and is finite in this instance. Definitions set limits (although there can be a process of developing definitions, of creating and molding definitions). The connotation of a word, on the other hand, implicitly means so much more than the explicit meaning. Connotation has no boundaries.

Let me give an example. The word is 'ecstasy'. In the popular sense or slang, ecstasy can mean something akin to fanaticism or hysteria/hysterical and in street talk, even the name of an illicit designer drug. From an etymological standpoint, it comes from the distant past. In Latin, the '*ex*' means 'from' and the '*stasis*' means 'place'. Further back, it comes from the Greek, '*ekstasis*' meaning being put out of its place, distraction, trance where the '*ek'/'ex*' means 'out', and *'histanai'* means to place or to cause to stand. According to Rollo May (*The Courage to Create*), "Ecstasy is the accurate term for the intensity of consciousness that occurs in the creative act." He calls it "suprarational" (as opposed to irrational) since it brings together the intellect, determination, and the emotions. 'Ecstasy' is the formal word, he tells us, for the "union of form and passion with order and vitality."

Nietzsche uses the word in the sense of 'out of place' when he says, "In the midst of all this life, joy, and sorrow, tragedy sits in noble ecstasy, listening to a sad distant song which tells of the mothers of being whose names are Wish, Will, and Woe." (*Birth of Tragedy*)

These are examples of the connotation of a word (in this case, ecstasy) which takes it beyond its etymological definition. The word finds meanings which differ widely depending upon its environment (time, place, or person).

Let's step back a minute. We want you to be excited about writing, but we recognize that it takes courage to change your ways and your opinions, to leap into something that has no rules, that is spontaneous. However, that's the point. Look at the word we just used: courage. What is its story, its etymology? Courage comes from the French word 'coeur'. Translation? Heart. Courage comes from the heart.

> "Courage
> is not the towering oak
> that sees storms come and go;
> it is the fragile blossom
> that opens in the snow."
>
> (Alice Mackenzie Swain)

So take courage. Explore, experiment, expand. Are you excited yet? Words carry so much charisma within their very core. Consider the etymology of another word; reveal. Reveal comes from the Latin *re* (un) plus *velare*, 'to cover', also from *velum* (veil) and thus, translates to; 'remove the veils.'

> "The hero journey is inside of you; tear off the veils and open to the mystery of your SELF."
>
> (Joseph Campbell)

Richard Strauss wrote an opera called *Dei Frau ohne Schatten* (The Woman Without a Shadow). I saw it performed in San Francisco in the late seventies. The stage was literally veiled from the audience, but as the opera progressed, one veil at a time was lifted. The audience became overtly aware of and involved in the drama being depicted on the stage.

One of my favorite words to research was 'text'. It comes from the Latin verb 'texere' meaning to weave. Think of writing as sewing a quilt. All the pieces with their various colors and textures are being woven together to form a beautiful spread. Weave your words. Remember e. e. cummings' poem:

> "anyone lived in a pretty how town
> (up so floating many bells down)
> spring summer autumn winter

he sang his didn't he danced his did."

Or:

"in time of daffodils (who know
the goal of living is to grow)
forgetting why, remember how
in time of lilacs who proclaim
the aim of waking is to dream
remember so (forgetting seem)...."

James Joyce was also known for his "stylistic pastiches." An anecdote that epitomized James Joyce's approach to the technique of writing goes like this: Joyce, while working on *Ulysses*, met a friend, Budgen, on the street in Paris. Joyce told his friend that he had been working all day and had produced only two sentences. "You have been seeking the right words?" Budgen asked. "No," replied Joyce, "I have the words already. What I am seeking is the perfect order of words in the sentences I have." Not everyone, of course, agrees on the artistic merit of Joyce's work (although *Ulysses* is considered by most as the finest written novel of the twentieth century). They become annoyed at the difficulty in understanding Joyce's 'vocabulary'. So, in their minds, if literature is to be a means of communication, it should be clear to the reader. Consider the following from *Finnigan's Wake*:

...or had topsawyer's rocksby the stream
Ocanee exaggerated themselves to Laurens
County's gorgios while they went doublin
their mumper all the time."

Or from *Ulysses*:

"Coffined thoughts around me, in mummy-
cases, embalmed in spice of words. Thoth,
god of libraries, a birdgod, moony-
crowned...."

It takes many rereads, but I believe it warrants
the time. Joyce will come through and start speaking
to you. Of course, his references and cross-refer-
ences may take a lifetime to comprehend, but I also
think that may have been his intention! However, for
more clarification, read Joyce's *A Portrait of An
Artist as a Young Man*. In this work, Joyce clearly
and lucidly writes about the "phrases of artistic
apprehension" corresponding to unity (*integritas*)
and harmony (*consonatia*). "You apprehend it as
complex, multiple, divisible, separable, made up of
its parts, the result of its parts and their sum, har-
monious. That is *consonantia*." There is a third level
or term he uses: *claritas*. "This supreme quality is
felt by the artist when the esthetic image is first con-
ceived in his imagination." The image, he says, is
luminous in the mind's eye "arrested by its wholeness and fascinated by its harmony". He compares
claritas to a spiritual state taking the subject of aes-

thetics to its highest level. This is the thesis of *Portrait of the Artist as a Young Man.*

Gertrude Stein, reacting to the way the Cubists in Paris were painting in the twenties, took her writing, like their canvasses, and moved beyond the limitations imposed by three-dimensional perspective. At this time, her writing was like a verbal still life but a still life in the Cubists' way of thinking or seeing. She attempted to capture the thought or the image at different angles simultaneously. The following is an example of Stein's explanation of her "experiment with language" and her way of explaining the skill and process of writing and maybe a little of that which only time and maturity can teach:

> "A sentence is inside itself by its internal balancing, think how a sentence is made by its parts of speech and you will see that it is not dependent upon a beginning a middle and an ending but by each part needing its own place to make its own balancing, and because of this in a sentence there is no emotion, a sentence does not give off emotion. But one sentence coming after another sentence makes a succession and the succession if it has a beginning, a middle and an ending as a paragraph has does form create and limit an emotion....

> "When I first began writing really just began writing, I was tremendously

impressed by anything by everything having a beginning a middle and an ending. I think one naturally is impressed by anything having a beginning a middle and an ending when one is beginning writing and that is a natural thing because when one is emerging from adolescence, which is really when one first begins writing one feels that one would not have been one emerging from adolescence if there had not been a beginning and a middle and an ending to anything. So paragraphing is a thing then anyone is enjoying and sentences are less fascinating, but then gradually well if you are an American gradually you find that really it is not necessary not really necessary that anything that everything has a beginning and a middle and an ending and so you struggling with anything as anything has begun and begun and began does not really mean that thing does not really mean beginning or begun."

William Carlos Williams, a poet whose writing was also inspired by the so-called avant garde paintings that were beginning to become popular in the twentieth century during the teens and on through the twenties and thirties, attempted to do what he saw the artists doing. He took inanimate objects and using language, gave them life. An example of this can be seen/read in one of his early poems, 'Winter Quiet':

> "tense with suppressed excitement
> the fences watch where the ground
> has humped an aching shoulder for
> the ecstasy."

When writing a story, think about a new way to look at the configuration of phrases. Reread the philosophy presented by Gertrude Stein or consider the writing philosophy of Aristotle presented in his tome, *Poetics*. Plot, according to Aristotle, "has a beginning, a middle, and an end; the roots of the middle are in the beginning; the roots of the end are in the middle, the end must complete what is begun in the beginning."

Question, always question. Compare Gertrude Stein and Aristotle's advice. Are they really so different? Do you believe life provides endings to situations? Do events simply blend one into the other? What about surrendipity?

We are constantly changing and growing, maturing and evolving throughout our lives. Our job as we grow is to integrate all these parts, all these influences on our lives. Remember, the full potential of the acorn is to be a mighty oak.

Inspiration can come from more than what we might loosely define as 'beauty'. John Constable, the great landscape artist, wrote that "[t]he sound of water escaping from mill-dams...willows, old rotten plants, slimy posts, and brickwork, I love such things.... These scenes made me a painter, and I am grateful." (from On the Laws of the Poetic Art, Anthony Hecht)

According to Virginia Hearn; "Nothing never happens." Use these objects for possible stimulation:

Umbrella   Teddy bear   muddy sneakers   picket fence

4

Music

"It don't mean a thing if it ain't got that swing!"

(Duke Ellington)

Poetry is "the expression, through human language, reduced to its essential rhythm, of the mysterious meaning of the aspects of life. Thus it confers authenticity upon our existence and constitutes the sole spiritual aim."

(written by poet Mallarme in 1886)

Some words are made up for the rhythm, the music, the sound. 'Primitive' (in quotes because our meaning here is rudimentary as opposed to intellectually inferior) cultures tend to be more in touch with the physical, the kinesthetic aspect of words. In Sanskrit, for instance, things are sounds. In our language, consider onomatopoeia. (Greek, onoma, onomatos, a name, and poiein, to make; hence, to make a name) Some examples: tinkle, buzz, chickadee, hush and meow. Alexander Pope (*Essay on Criticism*) stated, "The sound must seem an echo to the sense." My advice is to use this device sparingly.

"Music makes you feel hungry for more of it," said Toni Morrison in an interview. "Literature should do the same thing." Of all the contemporary writers, her work is on the top of my list for verbal musicality. Morrison not only recites the words of her black heritage but she writes in a metered frame, song-like when read aloud. She chooses simple vocabulary and chops her phrases to flow easily, chant-like at times, reminiscent of black preachers.

> "Here…in this place, we flesh! flesh that weeps, laughs; flesh that dances on bare feet in the grass. Love it. Love it hard. Yonder they do not love your flesh. They despise it. They don't love your eyes; they'd as soon pick them out…. And o my people, they do not love your hands. Those they only use, tie, bind, chop off and leave empty. Love your hands!…You got to love it, you!…More than eyes or feet. More than lungs that have yet to draw free air. More than your life-holding womb and your life-giving private parts, hear me now, love your heart. For this is the prize."
>
> *(Beloved)*

There is a certain affinity between musical rhythm and literary rhythm. Repetition of words and the recurrence of phrases make for rhythm. Even the placement of long and short syllables can produce cadence. For example, in Longfellow's *Evangeline*,

"THIS is the FORest priMEval. The MURmuring PINES and the HEMlocks...." The sounds in literature and poetry emulate nature. They can also resound with meaning. Rhythm is an instrument of art.

> "The creative act is not hanging on, but yielding to a new creative movement.
> Awe is what moves us forward."
>
> (Joseph Campbell)

William Faulkner said, "Life is motion.... The aim of every artist is to arrest motion, which is life, by artificial means and hold it fixed so that a hundred years later, when a stranger looks at it, it moves again since it is life." Words in themselves arrest motion. We, the writers, have taken the time to stop, observe with all our senses, the life around and within ourselves. We grab our observations and, to the best of our ability, convert them into words. We attempt to recreate life and so we try to make our words appear to move as life moves. Consider this wonderful sermon from *The Sound and the Fury* (be sure to read this out loud):

> "He was like a small rock whelmed by the successive waves of his voice. With his body he seemed to feed the voice that, succubus like, had fleshed its teeth in him. And the congregation seemed to watch with its own eyes while the voice con-

sumed him, until he was nothing and they were nothing and there was not even a voice but instead their hearts were speaking to one another in chanting measures beyond the need for words, so that when he came to rest against the reading desk, his monkey face lifted and his whole attitude that of a serene, tortured crucifix that transcended its shabbiness and insignificance and made of it of no moment, a long moaning explosion of breath rose from them, and a woman's single soprano, 'Yes, Jesus!'"

Read the poetic rhythms, the imagery, the emotional intensity (sorrow, despair, rejoicing) in this passage. This sermon was given on Easter in the novel. It represents not the Passion story, however, but the emotional climate of the Passion story: life, death, and the resurrection of Christ. Well written, words can do so much more than tell a story!

"To seek, beneath the universal strife, the hidden harmony of things." (Will Durant) This applies to readers and writers alike. Life is rhythm, movement, harmony as well as chaos. Our words should reflect all of these. Rhythm does nothing more nor less than enhance syntax. One of the most powerful mimes of life is sound.

Music soothes even the savage beast.

Many of the Baroque composers had a sacred belief in precise geometry within all matter. Their music was a reproduction of this. Baroque music moves the listener toward harmony, order, and inspiration. Listening to classical music also facilitates the thinking process. Don Campbell, author of *The Mozart Effect*, writes about his research on the effect that classical music has on the brain. Music somehow reaches our brain's intuitive area.

Music touches a part of the brain which causes our nervous system to automatically respond and react. A child with Williams Syndrome (where children have remarkably fluent language skills but have great difficulty with spatial tasks; have striking ability in recognizing faces but difficulty with problem solving; and have an average IQ of about 50) once said, "Music is my favorite way of thinking." In 1993, physicist Dr. Gordon Shaw reported that college students who listened to Mozart's *Sonata for two pianos in D major* (K. 448) saw their IQs increase substantially on tests of spatial-temporal reasoning—a skill related to math. However, the increase was only temporary. "It is not that the Mozart effect will make you permanently smarter," he reported to the Los Angeles Times in 1993. Hearing this music, he speculated, might provide "a warm-up exercise" for parts of the brain that perform high levels of abstract thinking. It was back in 1973 when a paper was written on brain theory that caught the attention of Gordon Shaw. Dr. Shaw had studied with Nobel laureate Hans Bethe and was an expert on particle physics. With the assistance of graduate student Xiadan Leng, Dr. Shaw devised a computer model to match musical notes to brain patterns and the result, although not Mozart, did match something resembling Western classical music. In another test, Dr. Shaw divided students into three groups. Using three environments, one exposed to relaxation tapes, one to Mozart and one to silence, the Mozart listeners saw their IQ levels rise as much as nine points. However, the increase began to dissipate after ten minutes. In 1998, Dr. Shaw co-founded the non-profit Music Intelligence Neural Development Institute where a curriculum was developed using a computer program and piano keyboard training to improve math learning. It is now offered in sixty-seven elementary schools. Dr. Shaw also published the book, *Keeping Mozart in Mind*. He died in 2005 but his work continues.

Mozart appears to strengthen the neural connections that underlie mathematical thought. Other researchers have used the two piano sonata to improve the spacio-temporal reasoning of an Alzheimer's patient and to reduce the number of seizures in epileptics. Here is one more example of how creativity (music in this case) connects the mind and body.

Bach and Mozart, not wanting their students' creativity to be devastated by repetitive études, created their own piano lessons. Bach wrote the *Inventiones & Sinfonias* and the *Well-Tempered Clavier* as enjoyable keyboard compositions for the student. Mozart wrote *Sonate Facile* for teaching purposes. The same analogy applies to writing and any of the other creative arts. To concentrate on the technical for its own sake will never produce a creative new work.

The Hungarian, Zoltan Kodaly (1882-1967), was another of many pioneers in musical education who observed the beneficial consequences when music was added to the educational experience of children. The music stimulated the intuitive side of the brain and the learning process accelerated.

Dr. Giorgio Lozanov, once the only psychotherapist in Bulgaria, moved to Austria to head an institute that continues his research in the scientific inquiry into the relationship between certain music and the learning process. Music acts, he writes, as a kind of transmitter. "As the phrases (in this case, phrases used in the study of a foreign language) were spoken in exact accordance with the tempo of the music, the music in a way transported the text into the subconscious mind of the listeners."

Progress is being made all over the world, the so-called progress called technology. However, as we have seen in music-thought research, another avenue of progress is also being made in the field of creativity. It cannot be ignored that the creative endeavor has a numinous (non-technical, non-scientific) side to it. Nor can it be said that creative work results from technical and scientific expertise. However, inspiration is an essential factor in both fields and its roots may not be as nebulous as they first appear.

Music has the power to revive myth. In music, there are no appearances. Music represents a plane of consciousness beyond form. It is the "metaphysical of everything physical in the world." (Nietzsche) Can you imagine life without music?

> "Music is your own experience, your thoughts, your wisdom. If you don't live it, it won't come out your horn."
>
> (Charlie Parker)

Silence somehow suffocates. Music triggers emotional response, joy and sadness, serenity and chills. Take the 'motion' out of 'emotion'.

> "Dickinson has a halt meter, like a hobbled horse or a Chinese woman who has bound her own feet!"
>
> (Camille Paglia)

Feel the movement as Faulkner describes a wave in the Yazoo River. "It reared, stooping; the crest of it swirled like the mane of a galloping horse and phosphorescent too, fretted and flickered like fire." Faulkner says that you, the writer, don't write to show your versatility. You write because you are human and it is inherent in your very being to render "the ageless, eternal struggles which we inherit and we go through as though they'd never happened before, shown for a moment in a dramatic instant of the furious motion of being alive, that's," he said, "all any story is." The emotion you feel is stopped artificially and emphasized by means of your pen or your keyboard so that the readers will see it as motion and feel in themselves the force and tension, the sweat and the agony, in short, the exaltation of living. That is the motion of life caught by the writer.

Robert Frost observed, "No tears in the writer, no tears in the reader. No surprise for the writer; no surprise for the reader." (*The Figure a Poem Makes*) Live life to the fullest. Open your eyes and see the wonder, the excitement, the clashes and clammers, the cataclysms, the movement of what we call LIFE. Let the music of life fill your heart and translate it with writing filled with tempo and beat.

> "It begins in delight, it inclines to the impulse, it assumes direction with the first line laid down, it runs a course of lucky events, and ends in a clarification of life— not necessarily a great clarification...but a momentary stay against confusion. It has denouement. It has outcome that though unforeseen was predestined from the first image of the original mood—and indeed from the very mood. It is but a trick poem or no poem at all if the best of it was thought of first and saved for the last. It finds its own nature as it goes and discovers the best waiting for it in some final phase at once wise and sad...."
>
> (Robert Frost)

Writing a poem, Robert Frost said, is "never a thought to begin with.... A poem begins with a lump

in the throat…a home-sickness or a love-sickness….
A complete poem is one where an emotion has
found its thought and the thought has found the
words…."

Art does not have laws. All that is required for
the writer is honesty and PRACTICE. Write, write,
and write until writing becomes second nature. Live,
look, listen and write. The magic is there inside
every human being. You may not even know what
you think about things you see and feel until you
write. When writing comes by *rote*, you will look at
what you *wrote* and be amazed. It is *magic*.

> "Writing is a concentrated form of think-
> ing. I don't know what I think about certain
> subjects…until I sit down and try to write
> about them…. Words on a page, that's all it
> takes to help [a writer] separate himself
> from the forces around him, streets and
> people and pressures and feelings."
>
> (Don DeLillo, interview in
> *The Paris Review* 1995, #128)

Listen to Mozart or Bach. Free up the waves of
images and impressions which are locked behind
our daily world of practicality and grind. Relax. Try
listening to the *Rondo-Allegretto grazioso* from the
Sonata in F Major for violin and piano or one of the
Brandenburg Concertae. Practice "earobics" for
awhile. Do not forget to have a paper and pencil
ready.

Consider the words of G. K. Chesterton, "The world will never starve for want of wonders, but only for want of wonder." With the music in the background, the windows of your mind should be wide open. Think of the pitch as mood. Think of the rhythm as pattern. Let your imagination flow! Now go ahead and write.

5

Imagination

"The imagination casts a wider net than the
actual net itself."

(Ryunosuke Akutagawa)

The writer needs to liberate the imagination of
the reader. The base word in 'imagination' is
image. Images call forth words to express
and reinforce themselves. Often the images remain
incomplete and words are needed to finish the job.
Abstract connections can be made; fantasies can be
completed; images can be fuzzy or fleeting or just
plain incomplete but words can render them free.
"Look to the image concealed within the emotion,"
(Carl Jung) and then transform it into art.

"Only dull and impotent artists screen their
work with sincerity. In art there is need for
truth, not sincerity."

(Kasimer Malevich, *Essays on Art*)

Let your words literally "spill out the truth". Let
your eyes and your mind's eye (memories) bear witness to your reality. The painting on the cover of this
book was done in just this way. At the end of day,
when I was painting a landscape, I gathered the

unused globs of paint from the palette and with a palette knife spread the colors across an empty canvas. A week of doing this and the canvas was covered with all sorts of colors and shapes. I turned the canvas upside down and sideways until I glimpsed images peeking through. Carefully, I allowed the forms to present themselves. Out came the Princess, then the unicorn, the old castle and the trees. All these were shapes and forms I had seen in Avignon at the Palais des Papes years before. They were there but they were not there. These images came from my memory (or imagination) and were just waiting to be expressed. Plato compared memory to a slab of stone. Nothing is lost through a lifetime.

Words reflect our human particularity: we are social beings. Within a single word may be contained a complete concept or a notion. First the words are spoken, even if it is in our head, and then they are written down. Once they are written, words go public. Writing is a dialogue whether it be private with ourselves or with readers. However, keep in mind, words actually create an audience by being written. To the reader, the word takes on a new and different form/image/thought/pattern. The author cannot control the imagination of the reader. The reader relies on his or her own past, his or her own memories to enhance the images and ideas provoked by the words. "Give what you have. To someone (else) it may be better than you dare to think." (Longfellow)

Sartre said in his introduction to Jean Genet's work, "The imagination represents objects to us in such a way as to incline our judgment in the direction we wish." Take the work 'represent'. Understand it as *re* (again), and *present* (as in presentation). The author cannot nor should he or she want to possess the words he/she has given birth to (i.e.: created). Once written, see the words as a gift, offered to the reader freely and without hitches.

Write about everything; the most trivial may be the most significant. Let the words flow; invent them if need be. Take for example the following piece from James Joyce's *Ulysses*:

> (A dog walking up the beach with his owners discovers the carcass of another dog washed up by the sea at Sandymount strand.) "Unheeded he kept by them as they came toward the drier sand, a rag of wolfstongue redpanting from his jaws. His speckled body ambled ahead of them and then loped off at a calf's gallop. The carcass lay on his path. He stopped, sniffed, stalked round it, brother, nosing closer, went round it, sniffing rapidly like a dog all over the dead dog's bedraggled fell. Dogskull, dogsniff, eyes on the ground, moves to one great goal. Ah, poor dogsbody. Here lies dogsbody's body."

Do you experience the dog's movement coming up to and then walking around and around the dead body? Do you see how the syntax and the rhythm work together to imitate the dog's movement?

Early in his chosen métier as a writer, James Joyce had attempted poetry and even theatre writing. Although his success came when he switched to writing prose (in 1904, the same year that he and Nora came together as a couple and left Ireland), he never forgot what he had learned about music (from the poetry) and drama (from the theatre), two natural states of mind in his native land.

Joyce took seven years to write *Ulysses*. His next novel, *Finnegans Wake*, took seventeen years to complete. Talk about fastidious! However, Joyce's work, in my humble opinion, epitomizes infinite patience, total commitment, and dedication. His writing represents layers upon layers of nuance, of historical references and mythological allusions, metaphysics, drama, and the universality of the most trivial things. To read James Joyce, I feel, is to experience the ultimate artistic poetic aspect of language. Joyce focuses on the message, the content for its own sake. The language calls attention upon itself. "When you read Joyce, what you get is radiance. You become harmonized.... It is not teaching you a lesson; it is feeding you. It gives you spiritual balance and spiritual harmony." (Joseph Campbell)

Look for patterns and pauses.

Consider the latter aspect of writing; the pause. What is not said is often more important than what is said. My mother-in-law, Georgeanna Lipe, is a painter and what she does is the same as what we are describing in writing as the pause. Georgeanna began as a medical illustrator at Vanderbilt. University in the thirties. Years later, she decided to paint with water color. This amazes me because it is what you leave out that is just as if not more important than what you put in a watercolor painting. From having to depict everything methodically as a medical illustrator to painting with thin water soluble colors where the paper is often shown peering through as part of the composition is an incredible feat. By the way, she is ninety-six and still painting.

First, let the words flow. Then when some time has elapsed (at least twenty-four hours), cut to the core. Often insinuation, implication, inference is more effective than fact. Hemingway apparently agonized over his 'one true sentence'. "Less is more" was his theme. As he said, "A writer's problem does not change. It is always how to write truly and having found out what is true to project it in such a way that it becomes part of the experience of the person who reads it." (Ernest Hemingway in Carlos Baker's *Hemingway, The Writer as an Artist*) Hemingway's method was to make long lists of words, often infinitives, to describe an experience. The lists were like verbal talismans helping him achieve what would end up reading or sounding like a total immersion "in the sensuous experience of living." Each and every writer must find a system or style which will make the vision flesh; a style which lets each image or story be born from a single pure emotion or, as Hemingway said, an "under-code" that allows a writer to create "the real thing, the sequence of motion and fact, which makes emotion." The predominant style of Hemingway is lean, pared, economical, and succinct. Faulkner, on the other hand, is flamboyant, rich, decorative, embellished, sometimes poetic, sometimes a hallucinating language full of texture and rich sensory impressions. They could not be more different; but then, are we not all, as humans, very different? The key to you as a writer is "to thy own self be true". Write the way you perceive and the way you feel.

Hemingway made some pertinent observations on esthetic principles in *Big Two-Hearted River*: "The only writing that was any good was what you made up, what you imagined…. You had to digest life and then create your own people." Writing he says, using the voice of his protagonist, Nick Adams, had to be done "from inside yourself…. He felt almost holy about it. It was deadly serious. You could do it if you would fight it out. If you lived right with your eyes." He says he knew how the painter Cézanne would do it, how he would paint the river or Mont Sainte Victoire over and over, but Cézanne was gone. As Hemingway stated succinctly, Cézanne just got old and, after working on his art all his life, he died. Art of any sort is a challenge and Hemingway respected the challenge; in his case, the challenge of being a good writer. "…but isn't writing a hard job, though?" he remarked rhetorically to Gertrude Stein. In the final analysis, Hemingway regarded writing as a *controlled personal mythology.* More on that later.

To paraphrase C. Day Lewis, do we write to be understood or do we write in order to understand? It is so often that a writer, be he or she a student or a published author, looks at the words which have spun themselves onto a page and says, "Where did that come from?" First the image, then the thought, then the word, it's magic! Remember what Hemingway said, fact plus motion equals emotion. Try Hemingway's exercise. It will help you avoid the common and annoying overload of adjectives found in much of today's 'lesser' novels and romances. Consider the message of Wei T'ai:

> "Poetry presents the thing in order to convey the feeling. It should be precise about the thing and reticent about the feeling, for as soon as the mind responds and connects with the thing the feeling shows in words; this is how poetry enters deeply in us. If the poet presents directly feelings which overwhelm him and keeps nothing back to linger as an aftertaste, he stirs us superficially; he cannot start the hands and feet involuntarily waving and tapping in time, far less strengthen morality and refine cul-

ture, set heaven and earth in motion and
call up the spirits."

This was written in the eleventh century! Now
it is your turn.

6

The Mystery

"But the artist appeals to that part of our being which is not dependent on wisdom; to that in us which is a gift and not an acquisition—and, therefore, more permanently enduring. He speaks to our capacity for delight and wonder, to the sense of mystery surrounding our lives; to our sense of pity, and beauty, and pain."

(Joseph Conrad)

Mystery is a truth so profound (deep and obscure, Latin, *profundus; pro*, forward, and *fundus*, bottom) that it is like a thimble tossed into Niagara Falls. And yet, we can respond to it. "Until we accept the fact that life itself is founded in mystery," wrote Henry Miller, "we shall learn nothing."

Writing is an art form that expresses this mysterious element most clearly. In this vein, Elizabeth Hardwick wrote "I'm not sure I understand the process of writing. There is, I'm sure, something strange about imaginative concentration. The brain slowly begins to function in a different way, to make mysterious connections."

There is magic in imagination; of that, I am sure. Take the base of the word and you will find 'magi' as in magician, guru, supreme and universal intelligence. We must learn to be receptive to the intelligence of the universe whatever form it may take. Reception comes when we learn to listen. That is the real meaning behind the pause in the written word we referred to in the last chapter. The readers need to pause and let our words speak to them on a personal level. We writers need to allow that pause to happen by not overwriting. With writing, just as in painting, it is just as much what you do NOT write/say/paint as what you do. Art demands that we let go. The irony is that we always make demands and want more and our mind races ahead. We are so speeded up that we tend to ignore what is here and now and close to us (emotionally and physically). Try to be present to where you are and to what you are doing.

They say that our bodies contain all the information of the universe recorded holographically. Did you know that if you break a hologram, every part, each piece contains the whole? But way before the hologram, Buddhists wrote of the Indra's Net. What is the Indra's Net? Read the Avatamasaka Sutra (Francis H. Cook: Hua-Yen Buddhism The Jewel Net of Indra,1977), the Buddhist analogy or representation of the concept of interdependent causation.

Far away in the heavenly abode of the great god Indra, there is a wonderful net which has been hung by some cunning artificer in such a manner that it stretches out indefinitely in all directions. In accordance with the extravagant tastes of deities, the artificer has hung a single glittering jewel at the net's every node, and since the net itself is infinite in dimension, the jewels are infinite in number. There hang the jewels, glittering like stars of the first magnitude, a wonderful sight to behold. If we now arbitrarily select one of these jewels for inspection and look closely at it, we will discover that in its polished surface there are reflected all the other jewels in the net, infinite in number. Not only that, but each of the jewels reflected in this one jewel is also reflecting all the other jewels, so that the process of reflection is infinite

The capacity of one jewel to reflect the light of another jewel from the other edge of infinity is something that is difficult for our Western, linear, rational minds to comprehend. Where would be the source of origin if all nodes are simply reflections? This where the creative side of the mind kicks in.

Then, using the creative mind, one could say that, in a sense, our bodies are holograms of the universe. In 1923, Rudolf Steiner wrote:

"If we try either through sculpture, painting, or drama—indeed, through any art—to
portray a human being, we endeavor to create a figure that is sufficient and complete
in itself—one that contains a whole world,
just as man contains the whole universe
within himself in his etheric body. For he
draws together the etheric forces from the
whole universe to mould his etheric body
within earthly existence."

The meaning of life is inside of each one of us.
The etymology is the word 'recognize' is to re-know.
It is already there, but often our hasty lifestyle keeps
it hidden.

Combine the two base words found in the multi-
syllabic word, 'imagination'; 'image' and 'magi'.
This is the combination which you carry inside
yourself; this is the mystery. Joseph Campbell
wrote, "The entire heavenly realm is within us, but
to find it, we have to relate to what's outside." See
the images. Express the magic. The German lyric
poet Rainer Maria Rilke (1875–1936) who created
what he called the "object poem" (an attempt to
describe with utmost clarity physical objects, the
"silence of their concentrated reality") pointed out
that "the world is large, but in us it is as deep as the
sea."

On the other hand, the more cognitive we get,
the more removed we may become from the instinc-
tive experience. Observe children and remember

when you were a child: so full of curiosity and awe. For the child, anything is possible. Universal truths speak to the child within. (Since the truth is very simple; otherwise, it would not be the truth!)

In schools today, students are taught numbers and words. The arts are progressively being pushed aside. They are considered less or not significant. "Rarer still is the institution at which a concern with the arts is consciously justified by the realization that they contribute indispensably to the development of a reasoning and imaginative human being." (Rudolf Arnheim, *Visual Thinking*) Imagination requires that we 'let loose': allow the creative urge to express itself. "A little boy wanted to fly, so his teacher taught him to read." (Sam Cornish, poet) Education is not something that the teacher explains. Learning is a natural process that develops spontaneously in the human being. The teacher can only encourage and provide the environment for this to happen.

Creativity is not confined to the artist. Without the free roaming of imagination, the scientist would never 'discover' new things and ideas. Einstein could never have formulated his laws of relativity without a dream. Creativity is essential for science. This is a relatively new concept. In 1901, Joseph Conrad, in a letter to the *New York Times*, wrote that, in his opinion, science is "not concerned with truth at all, but with the exact order of such phenomena as fall under the perception of the senses. Its conclusions are quite true enough if they can be made useful to the furtherance of our little schemes to make our earth a little more habitable. The laws it discovers remain certain and immovable for the time of several generations." Anything goes as long as the formula works. Referring to the sphere of art, Conrad stated, "[T]he only indisputable truth of life is our ignorance. Besides this there is nothing evident, nothing absolute, nothing uncontradicted: there is no principle, no instinct, no impulse that can stand alone at the beginning of things and look confidently to the end." For Conrad the two realms of art and science were irreconcilably contradictory. For him, fiction demanded a "spirit of scrupulous abnegation. The only legitimate basis of creative work lies in the courageous recognition of all the irreconcilable antagonisms that make our life so enigmatic, so burdensome, so fascinating, so dangerous, so full of hope." The mysteries of the imagination spurn categorization and formulas.

> "Whilst developing creativity,
> Also cultivate receptivity.
> Retain the mind like that of a child
> Which flows like running water.
> When considering any thing,
> Do not loose its opposite.
> When thinking of the finite
> Do not forget the infinite."
>
> (*Tao poem*)

Remember that the greatness of a creative work is not what it says or what it describes. The greatness lies in a writer's unique interpretation or vision. "Within each of us is a creative core that actively creates the universe." (Robert Hand) Go choose a special place. Sit still and just 'be there' before you begin to write. When you are ready, write everything you can about this place. Make the reader see it, feel it, smell it, and even taste it the way you do. Let your mind wander. Perhaps memories will float across your mind. Go ahead and let the memories flow. Let yourself tell you more about your self.

7

More Music

"I thought of myself as like the jazz musician: someone who practices and practices and practices in order to be able to invent and to make his art look effortless and graceful."

(Toni Morrison)

According to Pulitzer Prize winning columnist William Raspberry, the rules and the music of language are two of the most important lessons a student can learn.

The music of India has no beginning and no end. Music represents a plane of consciousness. It is going on all the time. Rhythm/meter/movements are instruments of art. To hang on or halt or cling to a moment in time is to disobey the rules of nature, the laws of existence, the essential rhythm, which is life itself.

Music is motion; life is motion. The challenge to the writer is to attempt to capture motion through the medium of the written word which will remain static on paper. A well-known writer once told me that sometimes when she was writing, the music of the words she was trying to shape and gather would take her far beyond the words themselves. "I am aware of a rhythm, a dance, a fury which is as yet empty of words," she said. In music, there are no appearances, no forms If this happens when you are writing, stop and be present where you are and to what you are doing. Find your own rhythm and balance, your voice and beat. The writing will come.

Toni Morrison, in an interview with Paul Gilroy, stated, "Black Americans were sustained and healed and nurtured by the translation of their experience into art, above all in music...." Certainly, Ms. Morrison, winner of the Pulitzer Prize for Literature, has captured the essence of black culture in her writing. Read her work aloud. Toni Morrison writes the way she hears the black voices. The structure, texture and tone sound like the indigenous and intrinsic nature of the black people she is writing about. After all, African Americans came from an oral tradition of story telling and song.

> "[I]t is only the story that can continue beyond the war and the warrior. It is the story that outlives the sound of war-drums and the exploits of brave fighters. It is the story...that saves our progeny from blundering like blind beggars into the spikes of the cactus fence. The story is our escort; without it we are blind. Does the blind man own his escort? No, neither do we the story; rather it is the story that owns us and directs us."
>
> (Chinua Achebe,
> *Anthills of the Savannah*, 1987)

Modern African novelists, like Chinua Achebe above, often introduce oral stories (song-tales, myths, folklore) into literature. However, oral tradition is not confined to Africa. Perhaps ninety percent of the New Testament is based on authoritative oral tradition. Native Americans continue traditions based on oral history passed down through the generations. Elsewhere, a study is being conducted on the oral traditions among ethnolinguistic groups in eastern Indonesia (East Nusantara Linguistics). In fact, there are more than one hundred oral traditions that are being researched (and thus continued) today as we begin the twenty-first century.

Let us see how we as writers and historians through tales of our own lives might incorporate the oral tradition into our writing. "To make the story appear oral, meandering, effortless, spoken, to have the reader feel the narrator without identifying that narrator,…and to have the reader work with the author in the construction of the book…is what is important." (Toni Morrison) Music and reader participation, these are two parts of the equation for a well-written story or novel. There is a certain affinity between musical rhythm and literary rhythm. The choice of so-called beat or pattern relates to content or the vision of the author. The sounds in literature are all connected with intellectual and emotional meanings.

Read the following passage by Ernest Hemingway out loud. Notice the cadence, the darks and lights, the alliteration emphasizing the soothing quality of the passage:

> "He lay flat on the brown, pineneedled floor of the forest, his chin on his folded arms, and high overhead the wind blew on the tops of the pine trees. The mountainside slipped gently where he lay; but below it was steep and he could see the dark of the oiled road winding through the pass. There was a stream alongside the road and far down the pass he saw the mill beside the stream and the falling water of the dam, white in the summer sunlight."

Hemingway's work is deceptively simple using active verbs and nouns. Most of the adjectives come from the reader. With the minimum of words, Hemingway could convey a view, a mood, and a place:

> "I heard and felt the canvas move as the man on the stretcher settled more comfortable.
> 'How is he?' the Englishman called back.
> 'He's dead I think,' I said."
>
> (*A Fairwell to Arms*)

In the following paragraph, attention is given to all the senses except sound, for this is a quiet place.

Notice the repetition and the unusual metaphor ("the logs...gray to the touch").

> "He sat on logs, smoking, drying in the sun, the sun warm on his back, the river shallow ahead entering the woods, curving into the woods, shallows, light glistening, big water-smooth rocks, cedars along the bank and white birches, the logs warm in the sun, smooth to sit on, without bark, gray to the touch; slowly the feeling of disappointment left him."
>
> (*The Two-Headed River*, Part II, a short story written for a magazine in 1925)

As the river flows, the reader feels drawn into the scene, lured as if he were being reeled in by the man's fishing rod. Then notice how, after the semicolon, we are back with the protagonist. It is he who is feeling better in his temple of peace. The river itself here (and in most literature and myths) represents transformation, rebirth, enlightenment for the person who attempts to cross it or enter it. This is an example of motion in stasis. The writer arrests motion (life) and arbitrarily chooses a moment in time in which to focus the story. Choosing a moment (in time, an artificial means of demonstrating motion itself) is as paradoxical as life itself. Faulkner's work best illustrates this notion. Consider the following imagery in *As I Lay Dying*:

"It is as though the space between us were time: an irrevocable quality. It is as though time, no longer running straight before us in a diminishing line, now runs parallel between us like a looping string, the distance being the doubling accretion of the thread and not the interval between."

Time here is spatial, not linear. The space referred to above is a river (remember the transformational experience?). Clearly, this passage represents motion in stasis. Time stops and the reader is invited to "come see". The essence of good writing style is exhibited here, a perfect example of consideration for the reader.

Instead of a writing assignment, I invite you to read Toni Morrison, William Faulkner or Ernest Hemingway. Read their words for the music. Read passages aloud. See if you feel as if you are part of the story. Look for the two elements: of music (literary rhythm) and reader participation.

8

Analogy of Painting

"Under this fine rain I breathe in the inno-
cence of the world. I feel coloured by the
nuances of infinity. At this moment I am
one with my picture. We are an iridescent
chaos.... The sun penetrates me soundless-
ly like a distant friend that stirs up my laziness, fertilizes it. We bring forth life."

(Paul Cézanne)

"I dream my painting, and then I paint my
dreams."

(Vincent van Gogh)

Georgia O'Keefe said, "To see takes time."
An artist never paints 'things'. The artist
paints relationships. He chooses a center of
interest and then considers colors, and their values.
Cool and warm, dominance verses subordinate. The
writer should also consider the elements of design.
Call it "effective visual paragraphing".

A writer can learn from the other arts. Consider,
for example, the work of Gertrude Stein. Living in
Paris between the wars, Miss Stein was in the midst
of a revolutionary movement called surrealism.
Based on the work of André Bréton, these surrealis-

tic artists emphasized the role of the unconscious in creative activity. Gertrude Stein, using this method, did not go after words, but let the words "come to her". Look at Picasso's artwork and the same thing happens.

Like Gertrude Stein, Picasso's original approach to art defied all conventions of the past (although he had already become a master of realistic painting when still in his teens in Spain). Unlike Stein, Picasso did not write but he 'spoke' with his art work. "One must never forget," wrote Gertrude Stein about Picasso in 1938, "that the reality of the twentieth century is not the reality of the nineteenth century, not at all and Picasso was the only one in painting who felt it, the only one." She continues, "…Picasso was the only one in painting who saw the twentieth century with his eyes and saw its reality and consequently his struggle was terrifying, terrifying for him and for the others, because he had nothing to help him, the past did not help him, nor the present, he had to do it all alone…." After 'playing' with painting, drawing, etching, lithography, wood and metal sculpture, Picasso, in 1946, discovered clay. Again he defied all conventions and brought fresh energy into the craft of ceramics. For Picasso, although it happened late in his life (he was born in 1881), this was just one more example of his unique creativity, "sculpting, modeling, and painting new shapes on traditional forms, transforming them with his metaphoric magic." (Suzanne Harper, Director of Art at the Museum of Arts and Sciences,

Macon, Georgia) Or as Picasso himself said, "When I was a child, I could draw like Raphael. But it took a lifetime to draw like a child.'

Vincent Van Gogh, when he had just realized his need, his desire, to commit to painting, wrote to his brother Theo, "Nature always begins by resisting the artist, but he who really takes it seriously does not allow that resistance to put him off his stride; on the contrary, it is that much more of a stimulus to fight for victory, and at bottom, nature and a true artist agree. Nature certainly is 'intangible', yet one must seize her...." Van Gogh was committed to *dégager* (seize from) nature the spiritual aspect or significance and share this 'reality' with others. In his view, this was the artist's responsibility. The 'calling of the artist' is to share that insight. In nature, Van Gogh said that he discovered "*l'éternelle*". In June 1879, he wrote, "I know of no better definition of the word 'art' than this: 'art is man added to nature', nature, reality, truth, but with a significance, a conception, with a character which the artist makes evolve, and to which he expresses, that he *dégage*, (clears, redeems, releases, frees up) illuminates (enlightens)" from nature.

Van Gogh used color in his paintings to express something internal. Talking about his use of color, he said, it is "not locally true from the point of view of the stereoscopic realist, but color (suggests) any emotion of an ardent temperament." Look at and study 'The Artist's Room at Arles' painted in 1888. The picture is less a portrayal of his room than a calculated analysis of an emotional experience. It is a study of complementary colors, blue and yellow, magenta and green, crimson and yellow. (This painting might also be considered a good example of subtractive synthesis when pigments 'color' by taking away colors.) Van Gogh was moody and temperamental as well as deeply religious and his artwork reflects this. He used thick impastos with paint applied directly from the tube. With his enthusiasm and impulsive nature, Van Gogh completed some of his paintings in a single afternoon.

His bright yellows represented love and faith; his blues (he qualified cobalt as 'divine'), reds and greens were passion. Consider also the symbolism of mixed (as opposed to pure) colors like orange. Orange promotes conversation and encourages spirituality. Green (blue and yellow) symbolizes relaxation as well as change. It encourages growth and feelings of tranquility and awakening. It was with color that Van Gogh attempted to "save others", to "stay the desperate and console the lonely". Translate this philosophy into poetry and we have a poem by Walt Whitman:

"Give me the splendid silent sun, with all his
    beams full-dazzling;
Give me juicy autumnal fruit, ripe and red
    from the orchard;
...Give me, odorous at sunrise a garden of
    beautiful flowers, where I can walk
    undisturbed....

Give me solitude and give me Nature and
   give me again, O Nature, your primal
   sanities!"

Van Gogh was a primary influence on Henri
Matisse who also used crimson, yellow, blue, and
green. But with Matisse's work, the paints are not
thick. They are applied in an almost watercolor-like
fashion. "Color was not given to us to imitate
nature," he said. "It was given to us to express our
emotions." But he too could have walked through
Whitman's garden at sunrise and observed the colors
in nature allowing them to speak to him emotionally. Then taking these emotional views of color, he
would translate them to reflect his own temperament
with a paint brush.

Paul Cézanne (1839–1906) is generally accept-
ed as representing the first 'modern' artist. Often in
his correspondences, he spoke of his "realization" in
art. It is a term of central importance in his conception of a goal for his work. "Studying the model and
realizing it is sometimes very slow in coming for the
artist," he wrote in 1904. Never daring to trust his
'acquired' knowledge, Cézanne felt that "the con-
viction behind each brush stroke" had to be won
from nature at every step. What he was hoping to
accomplish was to bring together the viewed and the
viewer. "I am still searching for the expression of
those confused sensations that we bring with us
from birth." His paintings reflect not only what he
observed but also the atmosphere and the emotions
he, the artist and the observer, felt while observing.

Still Life with Ginger Jar   Paul Cézanne

In the painting above completed in his studio in Aix-en-Provence (c.1890), Cézanne has spread out a basket of fruit, his favorite ginger jar, and various other things on a white tablecloth. All of these items are perched at various angels on a wooden stool. However, the stool isn't contoured correctly nor is the ginger jar looking secure. The angle of the basket does not relate to the angle of the jar. The whole scene is precarious and if we didn't know better, we would think this artist had not learned about perspective. Certainly this still life does not depict these objects realistically as they appeared in his studio. Or do they? The guide who took us through his studio in 1994 explained that Cézanne was attempting to place the viewer in the painting with the viewed.

In other words, the position of objects was determined by the way they looked as he, the artist (and thus we, the viewers), walked around the stool. His movement determined the contour and angle not only of the objects but the stool as well. Wassily Kandinsky in *On the Spiritual in Art* wrote about Cézanne's still-life: "He made a living thing out of a tea cup.... He raised the 'nature morte' to a height where the exteriorly 'dead' object becomes inwardly alive."

In his landscapes, Cézanne desperately wanted to bring to his canvases certain vitality, a force, a direct and personal expression to what he was looking at. Bringing form and color together into a coordinated harmony was essential (remember Joyce's *consonantia?*), but to achieve this harmony, Cézanne realized that he could not rely on his vision alone. His sensations were the key. This took him away from a static look at a mountain or quarry or whatever his subject was and led him into a kind of dialogue or dynamism with the atmosphere of the place and himself, the painter, just as he had created the movement around the table.

> "[T]reat nature by the cylinder, the sphere, the cone, everything in proper perspective so that each side of an object or plane is directed toward a central point...nature for us men is more depth than surface, whence the need of introducing into our light vibrations, represented by reds and yellows, a

sufficient amount of blue to give the impression of air."

For Cézanne, "the ultimate synthesis of a design was never revealed in a flash; rather he approached it with infinite precautions, stalking it, as it were, now from one point of view, now from another, and always in fear lest a premature definition might deprive it of something of its total complexity." (Roger Fry, *Cézanne, A Study of His Development,* 1927) We feel the pulsating energy of his strokes as he superimposes color on color and feel the reverberation of each new touch, a mental operation that was compared by Walter Pach to a musician "whose material…arrived much sooner at its purity as an agent of expression." Form in the long run ended up taking precedence over color for Cézanne. It became painful for him to eliminate or modify the physical structure of objects yet he continued on this path "making a constantly more rigorous elimination of the sensations which to him represented only accidents of vision and which were not essential to the new organism he was building up." This view of Cézanne's work takes the artist to a different level. It sees his work as something that developed apart from the artist and yet not really. For it was the artist's decision to eliminate this and that form or line and to allow the painting to take on a soul or spirit of is own. It was the call of the abstract conflicting with Cézanne's devotion to nature.

This dilemma is similar to a writer allowing the words to take over and dictate what they wish to express. You, the writer, almost stand by and watch in awe even though you know what is written all comes from you and your relationship to what is 'out there'.

Ultimately, Cézanne believed he could never reach his self-imposed goal and even wrote in his diary that it would be for the next generation of artists to discover.

And indeed, Cézanne did prepare the way for the next artistic movement to reach the art world: the cubists. Suddenly, to the two-dimensional canvas, a new dimension was added. Depth and distance had already been achieved and Cézanne had attempted movement, at least in terms of the artist's participation, but now a more complex temporal dimension was being added. This temporal dimension represented both the physical and psychological aspect of movement. Objects appear not as they are at any given moment in time but as they are seen from different moments in time and/or from varying emotional aspects. Study Duchamp's painting, *Nude Descending the Staircase* completed in 1912. Moments of movement are captured on one canvas. Not only the movement, but the element of time is captured as well. Compare this artistic form to James Joyce's concept of aesthetic arrest or 'stasis'.

Nude Descending the Staircase   Marcel Duchamp
© 2005 Artists Rights Society (ARS), New York /
ADAGP, Paris / Succession Marcel Duchamp

Another interesting literary comparison is *Absalom, Absalom!* by William Faulkner. Here Faulkner also creates the effect of seeing a situation from many different perspectives. This assemblage not only denies any one claim to absolute truth but also allows or forces the reader to search for something else which, at the very least, might approximate the truth. Like cubism, the narration is arranged and patterned on different levels. As we observed in the prior chapter (More Music), Faulkner's novels are spatial as opposed to linear constructions. Like the Cubists, Faulkner brings together different perspectives of an event and the reader/viewer is left having to decide for him or herself what the true reality is. In the paintings, the forms are taken apart to be reassembled by the viewer; the same holds true for Faulkner.

"Maybe nothing ever happens once and is finished. Maybe happen is never once but like ripples maybe on water after the pebble sinks, the ripples moving on, spreading the pool attached by a narrow umbilical watercord to the next pool which the first pool feeds, has fed, did feed, let this second pool contain a different temperature of water, a different molecularity of having seen, felt, remembered, reflect in a different tone the infinite unchanging sky, it doesn't matter; that pebble's watery echo whose fall it did not even see moves across its surface too at

the original ripple-space, to the old inerad-
icable rhythm thinking Yes, we are both
Father."

(William. Faulkner, *Absalom, Absalom!*)

Faulkner's novels are not easy to read. The
above quote, after all, continues, viewing and
reviewing and deciding and decoding until finally
resolving with a period at the end. Nor were the novels easy to write according to the author himself. He
once compared writing a novel to "trying to nail
together a hen house in a hurricane." So take heart,
dear reader, writing and writing well is difficult even
for the best.

"A work of art must carry in itself its complete
significance and impose it upon the beholder even
before he can identify the subject matter." This was
written by Henri Matisse in 1908 in his *Notes of a
painter*. "The whole arrangement of my picture," he
continues, "is expressive. The place occupied by fig-
ures or objects, the empty spaces around them, the
proportions, everything plays a part." Think about
these words in terms of writing. Everything plays a
part. Even what is not said, what is not described.
What is inferred or suggested is equally important.

There is a story which was passed down by the
students of an art school established in the nineteen
thirties and located in the beautiful Blue Ridge
Mountains of North Carolina. Willem de Kooning,
an already well-established avant guard modernist
by the 1940s (a member of a group in New York who

called themselves Abstract Expressionists) was to conduct a course. All the young students wanted to be in this great man's class. They wanted to learn how to paint abstract art. 'Professor' de Kooning let their passions rise as he was a good forty minutes late for the beginning of class. Finally, the great man appeared and with almost reverent, bated breath, they watched as he placed a bowl of fruit on the table in the middle of the classroom. "This," he announced, "is what you are going to paint." More than astonished, half the students were disgusted and left. After all, a bowl of fruit was generally the subject for beginning classes. Mr. de Kooning waited for their departure, cleared his throat and, the remaining students, continued, "You will paint this bowl of fruit until it is really there, on your canvas." More students left. "And then," he resumed facing the few remaining, "you will paint this bowl of fruit until it disappears!" The students who were smart enough to stay were delighted. Frantically, they began to prepare their canvasses, but, before they could begin, de Kooning had something more to say. "And then," he began, taking a sigh and clearly enjoying the moment, "and then, you will continue to paint the bowl of fruit until it comes back *on its own*!"

"Comes back on its own!" James Joyce decribed a similar process in *A Portrait of the Artist as a Young* Man. Stephen Dedalus, the hero, is speaking to a classmate: He points to a basket which a butcher boy had slung inverted on his head.

—Look at that basket, he said.

—I see it, said Lynch.

—In order to see that basket, said Stephen, your mind first of all separates the basket from the rest of the visible universe which is not the basket. The first phase of apprehension is a bounding line drawn about the object to be apprehended. An esthetic image is presented to us either in space or in time. What is audible is presented in time; what is visible is presented in space. But temporal or spacial, the esthetic image is first luminously apprehended as selfbounded and selfcontained upon the immesurable background of space or time which is not it."

Certainly, there are "phases of artistic apprehension" directly related to our view of what is 'out there' and the time we spend absorbing it. First we see and absorb the image. Second, we investigate how we relate to the image. And third, we writers or artists relate the form to others. It may take mountains of papers, hours and hours of writing, to come up with one true 'golden' phrase to describe that vision and that moment or as de Kooning says, to allow for the moment when it comes back on its own. All this we do as creative beings. So keep writing! Longfellow advised: "Give what you have. To someone it may be better than you dare think."

9

Participation

"Summoned or not, the god will come."
(Motto over the door of Carl Jung's house.)

I would like to return to the concept of the reader participating in the novel. Writing is a dialogue, writer to reader. The writer needs to liberate the imagination of the reader. When a story taps into archetypes (universal or 'perfect' types), readers will identify on some level. (The archetype is the creative dimension of our consciousness, according to Carl Jung. It represents the common thread that ties all humanity together. According to Jung, archetypes are intrinsic to man. They have been expressed in one way or another since man first expressed an abstract thought.) The story that best reflects these archetypes is called the myth. Sociologically speaking, a myth may be historical or fictional without altering its nature as myth. This is because the power of myth lies in the meaning and the broader truth it conveys, rather than the historicity of the story. The greatest attraction of the myth is its "secret opening through which the inexhaustible energies of the cosmos pour into human cultural manifestation." So began Joseph Campbell in his book, *The Hero With A Thousand Faces*. Since myths are about archetypes, stories and myths from all over the world are very much the same, from ancient times to modern day. Mr. Campbell saw myths as metaphors that "map the possibilities of our development from birth through maturity to old age and death, the possibilities of our relations with others, the development of nations and cultures, and our relationship to transcendence and the cycles of the cosmos." (John Lobell on Joseph Campbell) In essence, if we are true to ourselves, allowing the words to flow freely, then what will appear on paper will be our own personal mythology.

Heraclitus said, "Everything is flux." This is true of the reader's participation in the creative process also. The exchange between the reader and the written word (ergo the writer) can be equated with the constant unfolding of truths from the universe. Good writing can open the eye of the reader's mind allowing a better if not new understanding of the world and his place in it.

> "True wit is Nature to advantage dressed,
> What oft was thought but ne'er so well
>   expressed;
> Something whose truth convinced at sight
>   we find
> That gives us back the image of our mind."
>   (Alexander Pope)

Today, perhaps more than any other era, mankind needs the security of knowing there exists an order, a plan, a meaning to life. Creative writing is the food for the life of the spirit. James Joyce insisted, with some irony, that the the essence or true substance of man "consists in his being a conscious reactor against his uncertainty about having any significance." T. S. Elliot had said of Joyce's writing style that it was "a mythical method...making the modern world possible for art...." To Joyce, the aesthetic *was* religion. To quote David Lodge (*The Practice of Writing*), this fusion of art and religion was Joyce's "idea of the quasi-sacramental nature of the artistic process, the mysterious transsubstantiation of quotidian reality into something permanent and transcendent."

An artist is an artist, whether you are a painter or a writer. As a foundation, to be even halfway good, every artist needs two basic attributes.

1) Know your medium. We have already spent a good amount of time on the subject of words. Use them. Play with them. Read them and read them out loud. For example, if a painter is not fully acquainted with his or her medium, he or she will not be able to render the scene, person or object correctly. However, if artists experiment with and exercise the colors, the consistencies, the mixtures, the additives, the brushes, palette knives, they will be proficient enough and free to be able to paint 'as the spirit moves them'. Knowing these fundamentals, artists will achieve the color, the nuance, the depth, and the

consistency they want. In sum, the use of the medium will be second nature, instinctual. Only then can their focus be on the design. Only then can the creative urge be able to express itself freely. By the same token if you as a writer do not practice using words, you will not feel comfortable writing and your deep thoughts will not surface.

2) Take the time to notice each thing so each thing gets noticed. Compare looking with seeing. Recognize it as being the same as the difference which exists between hearing and listening. Write what you see and you will also write what you cannot see. James Joyce said that if we look at any object intensely, that object might become "a gate of access to the incorruptible eon of the gods."

To me, the most valuable aspect of writing, and creative writing in particular, is the process (not the product). The process is the writer's personal quest, forever reaching deep down inside his or her heart and almost always being surprised at what comes out, what appears on paper. The universe is truly both within us and without or outside of us. It can be said that there is nothing new in this world that is not old. All this the artist observes and records be it on paper or on canvas. (Note: 'Aisthis' with the 'ai' pronounced as a short 'e' means how you see things and differs from one person to the next. Thus, as translated into English, an aesthetic is one who looks at nature and translates it into an artistic form.) Understand being human and understand human beingness.

A spectacular example of the artist being pulled into his or her work by the creative muse within can be seen in the work and words of sculptress Essie Pinsker. Essie's works in marble, bronze and steel have been acquired by twenty- one museums around the world including the most recent acquisition of her bronze *Isaiah* by the Papal Chapel in Roudine, City of Peace, Arezzo, Italy. "My dialogues with stone and steel fire my creative juices," she writes. "And playing with pieces of clay can carry me from an abstract line into a direction that takes hold until images emerge and take form." Here the creative force takes over which she describes as "the moment when you become a vehicle for the infinite." When this happens, when the creative force takes hold, there is no stopping it despite the odds and obstacles. For Essie Pinsker, "Sculpting is an obsessive, arduous process where exhilaration and doubt are ever present. But I continue working, ever watchful for the creative spark that will push the piece forward and look for the moment when I can still the human need for resolution and let intuition propel me." (Visit Essie's web site at http://www.essiepinsker.com)

Try looking at a mirror. See your reflection. Notice that place between your eyes. No matter how you turn or twist, you cannot get away from being the central image. You see, you are the focus of your world. As a writing exercise, find a quiet place in the country. Sit down and listen. Feel your connection to what is around you. Being human is but one form of nature. Feel, see, smell, hear the bond you have with your surroundings. The universal, natural forces are latent with in you. Connect being human with human beingness. Now write.

Deerhaven Lake© 2005 Ed Knepley
http:// www.pbase.com/ed_k

10

Symbols, Math, and Nature

"Turn therefore from the common themes
to those which your everyday life affords;
depict your sorrows and desires, your pass-
ing thoughts and belief in some kind of
beauty—depict all that with heartfelt,
quiet, humble sincerity and use to express
yourself the things that surround you."

(*Letters to a Young Poet,* Rilke)

"In order to understand the universe,"
Galileo wrote in the 17th century, "you
must know the language in which it is written. And that language is mathematics."

"Nature itself is a symbol. It is a symbol in the
whole and in every part." (Emerson) The
Universe for Emerson was but the externalization of the soul. Thus, if we follow his reasoning,
the "use of symbols has certain power of emancipation and exhilaration for all men."

"The rounded world is fair to see,
Nine time folded in mystery:

Though baffled seers cannot impart
The secret of its laboring heart,
Throb thine with Nature's throbbing breast,
And all is clear from east to west,
Spirit that lurks each form within
Beckons to spirit of its kin;
Self-kindled every atom glows,
And hints the future which it owes."

(Ralph Waldo Emerson,
The Essay-Nature, 1844)

Let us go back to the history of man as we know it. Civilization began with man observing nature and making it work for his needs, his comforts and nourishment.

"The plants, rocks, fire, water, all are alive. They watch us and see our needs. They see when we have nothing to protect us, and it is then that they reveal themselves and speak to us."

(Apache Indian tale)

In the beginning, man lived much in the manner of animals, but, unlike animals, man had a brain, which allowed him to analyze and compare, and a memory to retain what he observed. While animals relied upon instinct, man relied on calculations. The biggest change probably occurred during what is known as the Neolithic period when man changed from hunter to farmer, around 10,000 BC. Land had to be measured for planting and fencing. Simple geometric shapes defined the areas; the shortest distance between two points was a straight line (this is pre-Boolean; it is earth measurement). With the construction of dwellings came the concepts of parallel, vertical and perpendicular lines. On a plateau in the Jordan River Valley lies the ancient town of Jericho (7000–4000 BC). This town was built during the proto-Neolithic period, the age of the beginning of food production and domestication of animals. Around 8000 BC, Jericho underwent a spectacular change. Houses were built of mud brick on round or oval foundations to form a new town. Eventually, walls were constructed for protection. By 7500 BC, the town had a population of approximately 200. Surrounded by a ditch and a wall five feet thick, the town was well fortified. Into the wall, the residents built a 30-foot high tower 30 feet in diameter. Considering the primitive tools, which have been excavated from that period, the construction of that tower was a remarkable achievement. Some understanding of mathematics was certainly a prerequisite. A book by Seton Lloyd, Hans Wolfgang Muller, and Roland Martin, (*Ancient Architecture: Mesopotamia, Egypt, Crete, Greece*, 1974) gives many graphic explanations of early architecture. Certainly, the pyramids of Egypt depict a vast wealth of mathematical genius and such mysteries as we may never understand. More on this further on when we discuss the significance of the triangle.

The word 'mathematics' comes from the Greek word, 'mathēsis' which translates as the way or method of learning, how to learn, and pertains to any science. The study of nature in ancient Greece was considered the pure science. Epistēmē is the Greek word for the way of studying which we translate as epistemology, the study of origin, nature, methods and limits of knowledge. One way of studying was via mathematics. One of the ways of knowing was with shapes and forms in two and three dimensions as depicted in spheres, cones, and cubes. The term 'geōmetria', the measurement of land, comes from 'gē' which means the earth and metria which is translated as measurement. According to Hermann Herkel in his book on the history of mathematics, as early as the fifth century BC, Greek geometry refused to rely on direct visual context. (We know that nature herself is not static. The Universe is fluid and fleeting, forever changing.) Rather, every proof relied upon a preceding axiom. In Greek geometry, the so-called discoveries were made using simplistic or symmetrical shapes. The Pythagorean Theorem was first illustrated using an isosceles triangle. But which comes first, the chicken or the egg? Does geometry exist in the real world? Can it be observed? Or is mathematics a figment of a man's mind created to fit and fulfill his intellectual curiosity?

This is how Werner Heisenberg (1901–1976) analyzed our approach to or our view of nature. "Natural science does not simply describe and explain nature; it is part of the interplay between nature and ourselves; it describes nature as exposed to our method of questioning."

Let us return to the Greek root word, *mathema*. 'What is learned' does not occur in a void. In fact, even the tenants of the chaos theory (which has come to represent that the universe is ultimately chaotic) are becoming aware of the actual uniformity of even the smallest particles which can be observed under a microscope. Pefection may not be readily observable, but in relation to shapes, it is observable using technology. What this all leads to is what began as observed data, then was refined and made uniform (and, therefore, in a sense, idealized) in order to satisfy theorems and formulas, has finally returned to the status of the observed.

Geometry is, as we have said, an area of mathematics which analyzes the properties of lines, angles, surfaces, and solids. Certain forms and shapes appeal to the mind. The ancient Greeks invested geometry and geometrically-derived ratios with 'meaning'. Take the 'golden rectangle' for example. It was used in Greek architecture (the

Acropolis); later it was endorsed by Kepler (the 'divine proportion') in the Middle Ages, and now it continues in many modern experiments. The golden rectangle awakens something familiar and pleasurable in the human psyche. Mathematics is an abstraction whose proofs rely upon logic, but in another sense, mathematics defies logic in its emotional appeal. Nor did Kepler want to be bound by the simple logic of mathematics. "I beseech thee, my friends, do not sentence me to the treadmill of mathematical computations, and leave me no time for philosophical speculations which are my only delight," said the great mathematician. Enthusiasm and imagination in service of speculation is what led Kepler to the discovery of his 'Three Laws' of planetary motion. Kepler's novelty was the fusion of physics and geometry. Considering his time in history, 1571–1630, this was indeed a creative act.

But back in ancient Greece, from about 1100 to 700 BC, man's knowledge about nature came not only from observation but from his desire to comprehend its innate sythesis of opposites, of harmony. These Greeks placed 'meaning' to various geometric shapes. For example, the cube represented kingship and 'earthly foundations'. The Golden Section represented wisdom and philosophy. The shrines to the gods were built using the Golden Section. The edifices for kings were more cubic in design.

In Samos, Ionia (Greece) about 580 BC, Pythagoras was born. Although clothed in mystery, this Greek philosopher, known for a theorem he inherited rather than developed (the theorem was probably deduced by the Babylonians 1000 years before, but Pythagoras was most likely the first person to prove it.) believed that "all relations could be reduced to number relations", a generalization gathered from observations of music, mathematics, and astronomy. According to Aristotle's *Metaphysics,* the Pythagoreans "supposed the elements of numbers to be the elements of all things, and the whole heaven to be a musical scale and a number."

Pythagoras founded a philosophical and religious school in Croton. The most important discovery made by this school was "the fact that the diagonal of a square is not a rational multuple of its side." The existence of irrational numbers challenged all formerly held beliefs. Philosophically, the implications extended further still.

Plato (427?–347?BC), on the other hand, had faith in the ultimate rationality of nature and believed that the key to understanding nature was to be found in the ideal, perfect world of mathematics. (Plato's writing, though philosophic, is very readable and stands on its own as a great literary work although it may be a compilation of philosophic writings from many authors.) The most notable student of Platonic thought was Aristotle. Going a step beyond the current philosophic ideas of his time, Aristotle stated that it was only through keen observation and experience that the secrets, the mathematical structure of nature could be understood and/or discovered.

As the centuries went by, scientific research enhansed art with its new discoveries. During the Renaissance, artists and scientists interacted. Anatomical studies and mathematical perspective made possible the accurate and realistic portrayal of people, animals, and physical space. Mathematics also allowed the artist to realistically portray a three-dimensional subject on a two-dimensional canvas. "The first object of the painter," said Leonardo da Vinci (1452–1519), "is to make a flat plane appear as a body in relief and projecting from that plane." The challenge to accurately represent an object or image was approached in the spirit of rational, methodical inquiry. Artists went beyond just observing nature and natural forces and began to instill ideal and intangible qualities to their art. Again, mathematics was implemented toward this ideal.

Mathematics is a tool. It creates harmony, from music to paintings to architecture. It is this aspect of mathematics which led Karl Theodor Wilhelm Weierstrass (1815-1897) to state:

"No mathematician can be a complete mathematician unless he is something of a poet."

Similarly, Poincaré wrote:

"The mathematician does not study pure mathematics because it is useful; he studies

it because he delights in it and he delights
in it because it is beautiful."

Another mathematian/researcher contends that
the beauty in mathematics lies in its stirring up
memories buried in the subconscious, awakening
these feelings to the conscious level of the mind.
Examples of this are: 1) the alternation of tension
and relief, 2) surprise at the unexpected, 3) the perception of unsuspected relationships, 4) brevity, 5)
unity in variety, 6) a sensuous pleasure, and 7) a
sense of wonder, even of awe. All seven of these
examples could be equally applied to the arts and
creative writing in particular.

Whatever our approach, it is universally agreed
that nature affects us: our bodies (physically), our
minds, (mentally), and our souls, (spiritually). We
draw from nature and in return, we become her eyes,
ears, and her speech. The trees don't know the formula, but, as in the case of the Dogwood, every
spring each flower is a perfect configuration of
quadrants, four matching pedals around a center
puff made up of tiny yellow balls. I imagine if we
counted the balls, they too would have the identical
number. Balls or circles and triangles, quadrants,
these reflect some of the speech aspect, translation
into symbols, used to describe nature. "The use of
symbols has a certain power of emancipation and
exhilaration for all men." (Emerson)

Let us look at the most common symbols.

The circle ● is the universal symbol of wholeness as unity. According to St. Augustine, the nature of God can be described as a circle whose center is everywhere and whose circumference is nowhere. Representing resistance and intensity, the circle encourages control, erudition, enlightenment, and the acceptance of endings. "Our life is an apprenticeship to the truth, that around every circle another can be drawn; that there is no end in nature, but every end is a beginning; that there is always another dawn risen on mid-noon, and under every deep a lower deep opens." (Emerson, *Circles*)

The cross ✚ is a universal symbol of relationships, of integration. The Christian symbol with the cross bar at the top quarter represents the death of Christ. The death of Christ represents compassion, passage, and eternal life. To the Buddhist, that same symbol might represent the 'I' being crossed out. The Buddhist word for this is *anatta*, meaning 'nonself' or selflessness.

To better explain this concept, I defer to Father Joseph Roccasalvo. Fr. Roccasalvo is a Jesuit Priest who until 1984 taught at universities and colleges in graduate and undergraduate programs. One such course, Freud and Buddha, was conducted at Manhattanville College where I was privileged to be one of his students. Since the mid '80s, he has devoted his time to his two alternative loves: priesthood and prose. His writing has been prolific including seven novels: *Fire in a Windless Place*, *Beyond the Pale*, *Chartreuse*, *Portrait of a Woman*,

The Devil's Interval, The Powers That Be, The Odor of Sanctity, a subsequent book of short stories, *Outward Signs*, and a play, *Waging Waugh*. Apropos the symbol of the cross, he writes:

> "I had experienced transience at an early infantile stage, and so learned the lesson of Buddhist impermanence before I could articulate it in Buddhist symbols; these, once discovered and internalized, made me feel I had come home. In short, I learned to be Buddhist by natural affinity and a Catholic Christian later, a priest—by conversion. The dialogue of Christ with Buddha is my internal conversation that never ceases.

> "The Christian symbol of the cross whereon Jesus was 'emptied' of all self was viewed by one Buddhist monk as the equivalent of the Buddhist doctrine of non-self, anatta, where all self identity is transcended; hence, the remark, 'Ah yes, the Cross, it is your 'I' crossed out.' One is at zero, the point of pure receptivity, for here the totality of being is embraced. In brief, 'you' are the works.

> "It's a religious version of the literary quest for the concrete universal in myth and symbol."

For another perspective on this subject, let's read the words of another author, Joseph Campbell. On the one hand, he was immersed in the rituals, symbols, and rich traditions of his Irish Catholic heritage; on the other, he was obsessed with 'primal' people's direct experience of what he came to describe as "the continuously created dynamic display of an absolutely transcendent, yet universally immanent, *mysterium tremendum et fascinans*, which is the ground at once of the whole spectacle and of oneself." (*Historical Atlas*, I.1, p. 8). Mr. Campbell traveled all over the world comparing sagas, stories, and myths. His conclusion from these observations was that we are essentially all one. In 1984, I was privileged to attend one of his lectures at UCLA. Standing quite inconspicuous to the side of the stage, behind a podium, Mr. Campbell was dwarfed by a giant screen onto which he projected slides. Sometimes he enhanced his talk with music. The story was and is always the same. It is the hero's journey. The quest.

> "The privilege of a lifetime is being who you are. The goal of the hero trip…is to find those levels of the psyche that open, open, open, and finally open to the mystery of your Self being Buddha consciousness or the Christ. That's the journey,"

According to the Joseph Cambell web site, "In his later years, Joe was fond of recalling on how

Schopenhauer, in his essay *On the Apparent Intention in the Fate of the Individual*, wrote of the curious feeling one can have, of there being an author somewhere writing the novel of our lives, in such a way that through events that seem to us to be chance happenings there is actually a plot unfolding of which we have no knowledge." Written by members of the Joseph Campbell Foundation, they conclude, "Looking back over Joe's life, one cannot help but feel that it proves the truth of Schopenhauer's observation."

Returning to symbols, consider the cross ✚ with each arm length equidistant from the center. This form symbolizes the need for collaboration, shared work and activities. In the negative, it can also mean fear of abandonment or a search for connections with others.

The symbol for the stability of life itself is the square ■. The square encourages security, and groundedness. On the reverse side, the square discourages conflict, nervousness, venture taking, and individuality.

To me, however, the most powerful symbol of all is the triangle ▲, a universal sign of attainment of goals, envisioning new possibilities. The triangle can also represent heat, activity, and action.

The world is three-dimensional. The third dimension is depth. Since sometime before 4500 BC, the number three has been recognized as symbolizing the spiritual aspect of life. It has also represented the ultimate spiritual being or God. "God in his state of resting within Himself is 1 in 3 and 3 in 1." (Elizabeth Haich, *Initiation*) The Bible depicts God as the Trinity. The Cherokee Indians symbolize the spiritual aspect of reality with the number three, a universal force which has intelligence. In geometry, the idea of 3 in 1 and 1 in 3 is represented by the triangle. The triangle represents perfect harmony especially the equilateral triangle in which each side is the same length.

In ancient Egypt, the pyramid rose up, a three-dimensional triangular form shrouded to this day with mystery. It has been said that the shape as well as the angle of the surface of the pyramid in relation to the forces of energy circumventing the globe cause this very energy to be harnessed within the pyramid. Dead carcasses have been found inside these structures but with no odor. Razor blades have been sharpened. Mummies have been preserved within a pyramid. Aesthetically, the pyramids are beautiful as their four triangular sides reach from a square base to a point reflecting the angles of the sun: the light at dawn, the brilliance at noon and the golden sunset. Yet how they could be constructed, with each piece of stone weighing close to 300 tons is a mystery yet to be revealed. (The Great Pyramid was constructed circa 2500 BC. How could workers using the primitive tools and methods of that era accomplish this feat?)

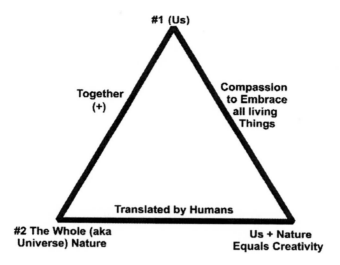

Consider the shape of a triangle ▲ symbolically. It has three sides and three points. At point number one, take the representation as self: you, the artist/writer. The second point represents what is 'out there': what you see. At the third point, the most important point of all, the representation is the result of combining the first two. Your relationship with reality (what is out there) is what becomes your art/writing/painting.

The Cherokee Indians have a symbol with a star in the middle. The star has seven points and ends with the number 9! How can that be? They start with the number 3. Why? Number one is myself. I know who I am. Number two is what is out there. I know that is real. Number three is the first unknown; it is the source of one and two: the Creator/God. "Apart from their belief system, perhaps the most valuable contribution of Native American spirituality is the insistence that the sacred power of the Universe must be experienced first hand." (from a sermon by Ed Piper, Minister, Universal Unitarian Church, Charlottesville, Virginia, 1995)

In a sense, as the eyes, ears, and mind of the Universe, the artist is God-like. When writing or painting, the writer/artist is the creator. The creation/art reflects something almost divine, certainly very special, not only about what is 'out there' but more important, something about the artist: YOU. Someone compared the process of writing to a spider pulling the silk out of its own body. You can never take the writing from the writer and you can never take the writer out of an environment: 'being there'. As Joseph Campbell said, "The entire heavenly realm is within us, but to find it, we have to relate to what's outside."

> "...[T]he true use for the imaginative faculty of modern times is to give ultimate vivification to facts, to science, and to common lives, endowing them with glows and glories and final illustriousness which belong to every real thing, and to real things only. Without that ultimate vivification—which the poet and other artist alone can give—reality would seem incomplete, and science, democracy, and life itself, finally in vain."

Walt Whitman wrote these strong words. On the one hand, he assumes that there is, in effect, an essence to things that transcends the merely physical aspect, and, on the other, that, for himself as an artist, a tremendous responsibility must be assumed; to share that insight. This is the "calling" of the artist. Whitman wrote the following poem ('Song of the Open Road') to reflect the relationship between the artist and what he sees and internalizes and finally expresses in his art.

"Allons! Whoever you are, come travel
    with me!
Traveling with me, you will find what
    never tires.
The earth never tires;
The earth is rude, silent, incomprehensible
    at first—
Nature is rude and incomprehensible
    at first.
Be not discouraged—keep on—there are
    divine things, well enveloped;
I swear to you there are divine things more
    beautiful than words can tell."

Ralph Waldo Emerson, born in Boston in 1803, also wrote about the relationship between man and nature. For Emerson, and as for all the Transcendentalists (a philosophic movement in New England from 1836-1860 including, besides Emerson, Thoreau, Margaret Fuller, and Bronson

Alcott), the Universe was seen as the externalization of the soul. I recommend his essays, 'On Nature', and, 'On Poets', written in 1844. In part, he writes:

"Nature is the incarnation of a thought, and turns a thought, again, as ice becomes water and gas. The world is mind precipitated, and the volatile essence is forever escaping again into the state of free thought…. That power which does not respect quantity, which makes the whole and the particle equal, delegates the smile to the morning, and distills its essence into every drop of rain. Every moment instructs, and every object for wisdom is infused into every form."

Language is transitive/transcient. (Latin, *transsire* to go across) Symbols too are fluxional. The quality of our imagination is this very flow. We cannot, as creative writers, attach ourselves to fixed objects. We must transcend the items and objects and allow the mystery to enter our consciousness. "Nothing is at last sacred but the integrity of your own mind." (Emerson) It is this very mystery, this inward subconscious level of thought, which leads us to use symbols. We need symbols. Perhaps it is true what the Eastern mystics say, nature follows man.

Consider the thought elements in perception
and
the perceptual elements in
thought.

Study the fractal on this page. Write about what this form summons forth or awakens inside of you. Let your mind relax and your thoughts wander. You will be surprised. Write about what you see and what you do not see. Widen your i'magi'nation and find the magic. That is your assigment.

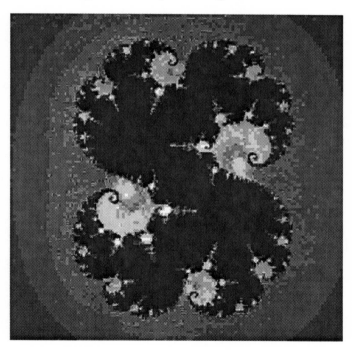

11

The Metaphor

"...[M]etaphor consists in giving the thing a name that belongs to something else; the transference being either from genus to species, or from species to genus, or from species to species, or on grounds of analogy."

(Aristotle, *Poetics*)

"My life in art is about an endless search for meaning. It's about a deep spiritual and metaphysical search to reconcile the human with the divine. The conflict is always between what is real and what is unreal. I never shy away from the absolute but seek proof in symbols and metaphors. My dialogues with stones and steel fire my creative juices. And playing with pieces of clay can carry me from an abstract line into a direction that takes hold until images emerge and take form. This is the moment of truth, the ultimate in letting the creative force take over. The moment when you become a vehicle for the infinite."

(Essie Pinsker)

The word, metaphor, comes from the Greek. *meta* means 'over' and *phorein* means 'bear'. Translated, it means to bear, carry, or take over; to transport. Grammatically speaking, a metaphor is a figure of speech in which a word or phrase that ordinarily designates one thing is used to designate another thus making an implicit comparison. Everyday language is widely metaphoric. To write metaphorically is to see likenesses. Kenneth Burke stated (in his 'Four Master Tropes' published in 1945), "Metaphor is a device for seeing something in terms of something else." Burke's research and concern was not with mere usage but with the role metaphor (and irony, metonymy, and synecdoche) played in the discovery and description of "the truth". Some examples: 'a sea of troubles', 'screaming headlines', 'an empty dream'. Metaphor is pervasive in our daily lives, so much so that metaphor can be said be powerful enough to provoke thought and action. For example, take the word war and see it applied in these conceptions of an argument. Your claims are *indefensible*. He *attacked* every weak point in my argument. Her criticisms are right *on target*. I *demolished* his argument. Try that *strategy* and I will *wipe you out*. She *shot down* all my arguments.

There is a mothering force to language and to the use of metaphors in particular. When you use language, you will find that it uses you. In fact, most often, it takes over and you sit back and learn from your own words. The vision of the thing perceived can be so much stronger when reinvented or reinterpeded by your memory of the thing or of the occurance. An analogy could be found in the story of Picasso and Gertrude Stein. When he was still quite young (in his late twenties), Picasso attempted to paint a portrait of Gertrude Stein. She sat for hours posing day after day. When he finally gave up, she pouted and who can blame her? But, in fact, he wasn't really finished. Picasso left for a short time and traveled to his homeland Spain for a visit. When he came back, he had an inspiration. Returning to his studio in Paris, he put up a canvas, arranged his oils and brushes and, from memory, painted Miss Stein's portrait. When he showed it to her, she was surprised. As her companion, Alice B. Toklas writes, "I murmured to Picasso that I liked the portrait of Gertrude Stein." But she was hesitant because it didn't really look like her friend. His reply? "Yes, everybody says that she does not look like it but that does not make any difference. She will." And she did...but many years later. In her book about Picasso which was first published in 1938, Miss Stein wrote, "In the nineteenth century painters discovered the need of always having a model in front of them, in the twentieth century they discovered that they must never look at a model."

Many metaphors are familiar throughout the history of thought (and "all history, properly understood, is the history of thought." R. G. Collingwood): the sun as wisdom; dark caves and ocean depths as death, evil and ignorance; water as life; the waning and waxing of the moon as death and rebirth. Consider bridges as well. All bridges speak the language of metaphor. Bridges are the stuff of legends and folktales throughout history. However, what is far more exciting about the metaphor is its unique character and its origin, both of which come from you, the writer's mind. As a figure of speech, a metaphor 'becomes' the 'other'. It is much more powerful than a simile. (Example of a simile: She donned a cloak of mourning like wrapping herself within a dark cloud. Metaphor examples: The wings of experience drove her forward.) Connecting two things or ideas in a metaphor adds a new dimension, another layer of understanding. Personification is a particular type of metaphor. For example, arms of a chair or legs of a table or 'the water cried out throatily to the landscape, I love you!'

Metaphorical knowledge transcends rational knowledge. Metaphor invites active participation. It is, therefore, not static but dynamic. In the Bible, Jonah is swallowed by a whale. "Now the Lord had prepared a great fish, and it swallowed up Jonah. And Jonah was in the belly of the fish three days and three nights." *(Jonah 1:17)* Metaphorically, a *fish* or a *whale* means trouble, difficulty and dilemma. (Consider how we say, when someone is lost in a city, "He has been swallowed by the city" and when someone is in a dilemma, we say "He is at sea," or "in the sea.") Metaphysically, *Jonah* means that prophetic state of mind which fixes man in bondage by his belief in the law of cause and effect. At that stage, it is believed error can never be redeemed or forgiven. (Refer to Charles Fillmore, *Metaphysical Bible Dictionary*.) Another biblical name, 'Abraham', translates as 'I am all'. The Bible is rich in metaphor. All the parables in the New Testament are built around metaphors and understood as such, so much can be learned for the text is rich with truths.

"Every myth is...psychologically symbolic. Their narratives and images are to be read...not literally, but as metaphors." Joseph Campbell teaches us to see beyond the symbols, lift the veil of illusion (maya). You are your own best resource for wonder and magic.

Life is a mystery, past meaning and definition. The "rapture" (to use Campbell's word) comes when we spontaneously discover or experience the 'ah ha!' "The world of life speaks within us when we let the active imagination function." The metaphor epitomizes this relationship between life (what we see and experience) and imagination. We must embrace life while we have the time and energy.

And as you read
The sea is turning its dark pages
Turning
Its dark pages.

(Denise Levertov)

Carl Gustav Jung translated John 3:3-7 as "And Jesus said to Nicodemus: Do not think carnally, or you will be flesh, but think symbolically, and then you will be spirit." The key is to allow your thoughts to become realities on their own. Combine your experience, your education with what you perceive today/now. Out of this mixture may evolve something new, a possible metaphor to transport you to the level of the spirit.

Analogy, the basis of metaphor, relates the temporal to the transcendent. Thus metaphors can be rich far beyond their rationale. To use Joseph Campbell's example, you describe Jack as running fast with the following sentence; 'Jack is a deer.' This metaphorical knowledge about Jack transcends rational knowledge. This is Jack's 'mythic reality, a psychologically compelling symbol of the person Jack.

There can be an amusing side to metaphors and similes. One of my favorite writers is Tom Robbins. I invite you to enjoy some lines from *skinny legs and all*: First the simile:

> "Like a neon fox tongue lapping up the powdered bones of space chickens, the rising sun licked away the light snow that had fallen during the night."

Then the metaphor:

"It was a bright, defrosted, pussy-willow day at the onset of spring, and the newly-weds were driving cross-country in a large roast turkey."

I won't explain that one; I just hope it entices you to read the book. At the very least, the exposure might enhance your own writing. Coming up with metaphors can be fun, but do remember, it can also be enlightening. Now let your imagination take you for a ride.

12

Myth

"…[M]yth is the secret opening through which the inexhaustible energies of the cosmos pour into human cultural manifestation."

(Joseph Campbell)

The habit of telling stories is one of the most primitive traits of the human race. The earliest myths were simply a way of explaining death, birth, the sun, the thunder, the world as it was observed. In these early myths, natural forces were not personified, the storm or ocean or disease was a person, a divinity. In Greek, *mythos* means 'fable', 'talk', 'speech'. By the time the myth came to the more evolved civilization of Greece, man had come to recognize his separateness. The myth became religion. As the eminent scholar of comparative religions, Mircea Eliade, states in *Myths, Rites, Symbols*, in sacred societies, myths gave "meaning and value to life." In fact, the narrative poet, Homer, was the first to admit to feelings and emotions as belonging to him or his characters and not emanating from the gods (although like Socrates and Buddha, he may represent many poets since nothing has been handed down that was written by him).

For thinkers like Eliade and Carl Jung and Joseph Campbell, myths are far more than fiction; they are real and necessary and very significant to the human psyche and the human race. Ultimate reality is irrational, beyond reason, and is justified by myth, according to Friedrich Nietzsche, a German philosopher who lived from 1844 to 1900. He wrote, "...myth can itself only be defined in terms of the constant elimination of definitions." Myth both reveals and conceals, an arbitrary and ironic sort of thing. It resides in an intermediary state between the conscious/real/fact and the subconscious/dream/potential. It is beyond the confines of time and space. It is cyclical as opposed to linear. It is through myths that the world is justified as an aesthetic phenomenon. (Remember that *aisthetes* is the Greek word meaning 'one who perceives'.) Soren Kierkegaard (1813–1855), Danish philosopher and writer of religious themes, stated it this way, "The mythical is...the enthusiasm of the imagination in the service of speculation.... We have need of myth for the enchantment of the soul." The subject of myth is at once true and not true. The object of myth is to explain the unknown.

Myth also satisfies the emotions (and the emotions must be satisfied if the intellect is to be convinced!). "To transform the external world into the inner domain of the psyche is the role of myth." (Karl Reinhard) Birth, death, love, guilt, quests, rebirth—these are all the stuff, the essence, of myth.

Myths are the archetypes, the emotional patterning, whose unconscious charge can stir and disturb us.

Facts and reason cannot ultimately define what is real. Myths were created to explain what could not be rationally defined or understood. The myth is the story of that common thread that ties us together as humanity and which binds us to the world in which we live. It is real in that it relates to the world; it is unreal in that it requires the imagination to comprehend. Mythology allows the mind to participate in an abstract field, a field full of intense meaning. History and psychology come into play in mythology although Nietzsche felt that Greek myths died when they took on historical significance. What is valuable, however, is the process not the result, the creating not the created. Myth encompasses all this. The myth is a story which is dreamlike, being poetic, philosophical, historical and even religious. Myth tells a story, a story that is dreamlike being both real and unreal. Read Joseph Conrad's *Heart of Darkness*. The novel is multi-layered, philosophical, abstract, but also entertaining, interesting, and stimulating. While following more or less a story line, the novel is more concerned with asking questions than in providing answers. On one level, it is sheer myth.

> "It was as though a veil had been rent. I saw
> on that Ivory face the expression of somber
> pride, of ruthless power, of craven terror—
> of an intense and hopeless despair. Did he

live his life again in every detail of desire, temptation, and surrender during that supreme moment of complete knowledge?"

It was at this moment in the novel that Kurtz cried, "The horror! The Horror!" Then he died. In essence, the story symbolizes Conrad's concern for man's place in the "tremendousness of the universe" as his protagonist, Mr. Kurtz, takes a "night journey" into the savage heart of Africa only to discover the darkness of his own soul.

Carl Jung (1875-1961) who was blessed with a long life was also cursed to live to see what the human race was doing to itself. He viewed this period as "an age filled with apocalyptic images of universal destruction." The 'iron curtain', the hydrogen bomb, State absolutism, all these were threats and he was concerned, so concerned that in 1957 he wrote, "Is [man] capable of resisting the temptation to use his power for the purpose of staging a world conflagration?...Does he know he is on the point of losing the life-preserving myth of the inner man which Christianity has treasured up for him?" It is the individual acting on his own initiative, he affirms, who is the "makeweight that tips the scales." He affirmed that he was "neither spurred on by excessive optimism nor in love with high ideals, but merely concerned with the fate of the individual human being - that infinitesimal unit on whom a world depends, and in whom, if we read the meaning of the

Christian message aright, even God seeks his goals."
To counter the possibility of destruction, therefore,
Jung affirms that man can overcome malice and
resist the dominance of evil, by affirming his individuality, his "self-knowledge". To some these
words would come across as slander, but to others, it
would be right and appropriate when Jung asks us,
the people of today, to understand the symbolism of
what he calls "the Christian mythology". Be assured,
he is by no means demeaning the Christian faith.
"The objection that understanding [Christianity]
symbolically puts an end to the Christian's hope of
immortality is invalid, because long before the coming of Christianity, mankind believed in a life after
death...." He continues, "The danger that a mythology understood too liberally, and as taught by the
Church, will suddenly be repudiated lock, stock and
barrel is today greater than ever." (Remember, this is
being written in 1957.) "Is it not time," he asks, "that
the Christian mythology, instead of being wiped out,
was understood symbolically for once?" (For more
information on this topic read Jung's *The
Undiscovered Self [Past and Future]*; in particular,
the Chapter, The Plight of the Individual in Modern
Society.)

Let us return to the discussion and understanding of the mythical concept itself. Myths epitomize
movement as they flow with illusion and change.
Myth is always becoming. It is never static. Today,
according to Nietzsche, "stripped of myth, (man)
stands famished (within) his past and must dig fran-

tically for roots…." Joseph Campbell, in his book, *A Hero With A Thousand Faces,* also laments the lack of myth in the modern world. "The world formulated is aesthetic not logical. It calls for the creative process within man."

James Joyce had his opinions about myth and man's relationship with myth. As an example he talks about eating lunch. You or I do this every day. Somehow that lunch is digested. But do any of us know consciously how we digest that lunch? But we will be doing it; that is how the body works. So it is understood that there is much more to each of us than our mental consciousness knows about or understands. "The vocabulary that relates and links our mental consciousness to the energies that inform our body and move our lives and give us sentiments of love and hate and despair is the vocabulary of myth." This idea can be applied as well to other non-physical ideas and actions as well. Take for example the concept of compassion. The feeling of compassion "releases you from ego orientation." Suddenly you are aware of a oneness with another. It is the opposite of what Nietzsche calls the *principium individuationis* which comes as a result of the separating factors of time and space. The actual realization of identity with another, however, happens and perhaps it only happens rarely, but when it does, it too is a true experience and, dare we say, it is an expression of that inward light, the realization of the creative muse's environment.

Myth, Magic, and Metaphor

In his wonderful poem about the mythical figure, Paul Bunyan, W. H. Auden wrote:

"A man is a form of life that dreams in
order to act
And acts in order to dream."

Keep a journal. C.S. Lewis did. "...I used my own pen to probe my own wound," he wrote. The journal represents in words our journey through life. The journal process frees us to slow down. Re-learn contemplation. Write about what you see but also write about what you cannot see. The greatest satisfaction comes when we discover from our own words what we were not aware of before we began to write. "It is out of what I don't know that I begin to write." (Toni Morrison) Create or discover your own myths. Gertrude Stein pointed out that "there's no point in roots if you can't take them with you." Memory is a root into recalled stories of our past. Our personal histories are also narrative histories. Feel your connection to the past and to the future. We are all part of the continuum.

"A diarist is a writer who watches himself
watching himself."

(Edward Robb Ellis)

Preserve the past for the future. Write your story, share your observations. Write about everything: your first love, a bad teacher, your father's yelling at you when you fell off the bicycle he gave to you. These stories all tell about you and more. They tell about a time and place and person from the past. How else will the next generation learn about what came before? We certainly cannot rely on email! So many great ideas lost to the click of a mouse.

13

The Process

The process of writing evokes "that emotion definite and physical and yet nebulous to describe: the ecstasy, that eager and joyous faith and anticipation of surprise which the yet unmarred sheet beneath my hand held inviolate and unfailing, waiting for release."

William Faulkner

The most valuable aspect of writing, creative writing in particular, is the process, not the product. It is the journey, not the destination; the creating, not the created. Nancy Willard wrote, "I haven't a clue as to how my story will end. But that's all right. When you set out on a journey and night covers the road, you don't conclude that the road has vanished. And how else could you discover the stars?"

Phyllis Whitney told me that she has no preconceived story. When she writes a mystery novel, she said, she begins with the place. Traveling to a specific location, she gets to know the place intimately. Then she creates some characters and gets to know them. They develop personalities and speak to her and to each other while she listens. Finally the plot begins. When asked if she knows ahead or plans ahead who did the crime or what will happen, she laughs and says, "Of course not! I have to wait just like the rest of you to find out!" (Paraphrased from a conversation I had with the author in Charlottesville, Virginia.)

Toni Morrison noted that there is an art to writing well which requires thrift, choosing just the right words and giving a sense of being there, plus a real yearning:

> "I was always conscious of the constructed aspect of the writing process, and that art appears natural and elegant only as a result of constant practice and awareness of its formal structures. You must practice thrift in order to achieve that luxurious quality of wastefulness...."

The structure is important. It is the foundation. The "thrift" is only achieved when you have allowed the words to flow and then return to find that golden phrase, that spark of insight, the flash of understanding. There is the letting go, the expression of your creative muse, that will only come as you write and write and write, much and often.

Rudyard Kipling spoke of the Daemon who "was with me in the Jungle books and both Puck books" and why he had to take great care "to walk delicately lest he should withdraw." He warns the writer, "When your Daemon is in charge, do not try to think consciously. Drift, wait and obey."

There are so many avenues to explore and every writer must find his or her own. However, one thing is true about all artists and writers, they are endlessly inventive.

Look for the extraordinary in the ordinary (take the 'order' out of 'ordinary'). Some things happen with an uncanny order called serendipity. An example of this happened to Scarlotti. A cat jumped on his piano and played notes. Scarlotti composed these very notes and created a beautiful fugue (*Cat's Fugue*). The discovery of Penicillin was serendipitous also. Life is like that. Behind what appears as choas or without meaning, there is, nevertheless, some kind of order. Even the mathematical interpretation of the Chaos Theory (Chapter 10, Symbols Math & Nature) has discovered a new order in fractals. Thanks to computers, we can visualize fractals. A fractal shape has a repetitive pattern which gives it a beautiful or pleasant aesthetic appeal. (For a better and compreshensive under standing of 'chaos' I refer you to Stephen Hawking's work).

It has been said that to forget the past is to rob the future. The world is changing so rapidly as we are being transformed by globalism as well as terrorism. (As Thomas L. Friedman writes, in the twenty-first century, the world is flat. As our lines of communication connect us "which requires us to run faster in order to stay in place", we need to let our imagination act, have free rein, and then to act on our imagination.) It would be well to concentrate on what we all have in common and share our ideas in the spirit of hope for peace throughout the world.

We can learn from the past. Since history can be said to be nothing other than some else's point of view, let your view count and help our children and grandchildren learn and grow. So, let me reinforce my plea, keep a journal. Some incident may seem commonplace but, upon reflection (etymology: 'bending back'), you may find it illuminating (charged with inner meaning/light). After all, "Nothing never happens." (Virginia Hearn) W. H. Auden said, "How do I know what I think until I see what I say!" You too may be amazed and the world may become a better place for it.

> "Writing is like a raft that buoys me above the waters of my life, not to keep me from having to swim, but to allow me to gather my breath, plunge deeper and delve for greater riches, then return to the raft and warming, to study and enjoy what I have found on the ocean floor."
>
> (Alice Helen Masek)

14

Reading and Writing, It's Therapy!

Poem finding a path

The words stick in the teeth.
Rich and boiling, ideas copulate
with syllables, generate, bubble
inwardly upward, unhindered
until they reach the traffic jam
at the junction of brain, breath, tongue.
There in the gullet they clot, flatten,
turn hard and dull. Wrong pieces
mate and will not come unstuck.
Shards of images, the sentences
stick in the teeth
or issue in an awkward belch,
disturbing the peace
unless they find an alternate
escape route. Somehow the joints
of shoulder, elbow, wrist,
present no obstacle. Along
striated nerves and muscles, the blips
of light and color dance and flow
smoothly, string themselves
on an iambic thread, slip.
their enamel down the arm

via ink, assemble, establish
themselves according to their
innate poetry, form rows
and stand up to be read.

Luci Shaw, *Polishing the Peroskey Stone*

Cadmus defended writing in rebuttal to Hercules. "I taught Greece the art of writing," he said. "You (Hercules) subdued monsters; I civilized men. It is from untamed passions, not from wild beasts, that the greatest evils arise to human society. The genuine glory, the proper distinction of the rational species, arises from the perfection of the mental powers.... Unhappy are the people who are governed by valor not directed by prudence, and not mitigated by the gentle arts." (Source unknown) Aristotle had said that, in his opinion, poetry was more philosophical than history since poetry dealt with the universal and history with the unique facts or epics, i.e. the particular.

For the artist, writer or musician, the beauty of nature reflects clarity and order. Our participation in and with nature allows us to recognize that fact. The universe is truly both within and without each one of us. There is nothing new that is not old. All this, the artist observes and records.

"Learn to get in touch with silence within yourself, and know that everything in this life has a purpose. There are no mistakes,

no coincidences, all events are blessings
given to us to learn from."

(Elisabeth Kübler-Ross, 1926–2004)

To be an artist or a writer is not a matter simply of making paintings or writing. It is a state of consciousness. It is the shape of our perception.

An essential learning tool for good writing may be obtained with no effort at all. It is called exposure. Read good literature. Jacques Barzun, wrote *Simple & Direct, A Rhetoric for Writers.* This is one of those mandatory books to keep with you when you are writing, along with the Encyclopedia Britannica, a Roget's Thesaurus, Word Finder, the Webster's Unabridged Dictionary, Volumes I and II as well as the latest edition of *SPELL/Binder* published by the Society for the Preservation of the English Language and Literature. In his closing paragraph, Barzun states, "Reading abundantly, in good books, is indispensable. It is only in good writing that you will find how words are best used, what shades of meaning they can be made to carry, and by what devices (or lack of them) the reader is kept going smoothly or bogged down in confusion."

Read mythologies. "For mythology is the handmaiden of literature; and literature is one of the best allies of virtue and promoters of happiness. Without knowledge of mythology much of the elegant literature of our own language cannot be understood and appreciated." (*Bulfinch's Mythology*, Introduction) The feelings both positive and negative of an individual are, when reduced to their simplest form, the same as feelings that have been expressed throughout the ages via the myth. Read Carl Jung and his analysis of 'the collective unconscious' (what he calls 'archetypes'). It is through our emotions that we recognize ('re-know') our unity as members of the human race. Nietzsche said, "Without myth, every culture loses its healthy and creative natural process." We need to share our sameness with our fellow man: the future of the planet depends on it. So read and find the myths in literature, but also find the literature in myths.

> "The latest incarnation of Oedipus, the continued romance of Beauty and the Beast, stand this afternoon on the corner of Forty-second Street and Fifth Avenue, waiting for a traffic light to change."
>
> (Joseph Campbell)

Open your eyes and you will see myths everywhere. The more you read, the more you will see and the more you see, the more you will have to write about.

Do not worry about imitation. Your own writing will, of course, respond to and reflect what you have read. However, as long as you retain your own 'voice', what you have read will only enhance and add to your own work.

There is no Frigate like a Book

To take us lands away
Nor any Coursers like a Page
Of Prancing Poetry.
This Traverse may the poorest take
Without oppress of Toll—
How frugal is the Chariot
That bears the Human Soul.

(Emily Dickinson)

Rita Dove, poet Laureate and English professor at the University of Virginia, told a group of school children that she "loved to talk to books." She recited a list of classics like *Treasure Island*, *King Arthur*, *Kidnapped*, and *Robinson Crusoe*. "Those books contained within them worlds within worlds. They were windows of the imagination."

Ray Bradbury, truly a living legend, writer of short stories, film maker, playwright, screen writer, and one of America's greatest raconteurs, came to San Diego, California, and encouraged his audience of writers and would be writers to go to the library. Live in the library. Go and fall in love. Love authors like Jules Verne, Herman Melville, Rudyard Kipling, Thomas Wolfe, Emily Dickinson, Ernest Hemingway, F. Scott Fitzgerald. Make your own list but read good literature not what is on the best seller list. Go to the library and read about your senses, he said. Read about your eyes. Read about your ears. Collect metaphors. All of this reading will help you develop your own metaphors. Study Haiku; it is all metaphor. Mr. Bradbury says that the Old Testament and Shakespeare "were his midwives." They birthed him in metaphor. Remember, he said, "you collect things intuitively not intellectually." His audience was advised to "remember when you were a child, eleven, twelve, or fifteen, and a good book would transport you into another world and you ran and told everybody you knew that they had to read this book?" His advice? Never loose that enthusiasm.

"The one thing we seek with insatiable desire," wrote Emerson, "is to forget ourselves, to be surprised out of propriety, to lose our sempiternal [having neither beginning nor end; eternal] memory, and to do something without knowing how or why.... Nothing great was ever achieved without enthusiasm."

Continue to fall in love with great authors and great books. We are never going to know the secret of life. Darwin, the Old Testament, the Koran, the Creationists, take a little from each. The important thing is to get on with "the elation of living." Witness and celebrate life. Take a chance. Make a difference.

Reading and writing are like taking in the wonders of the world and handing them back out again. If a book is going to be successful, it will stimulate the reader emotionally. If the writing is going to be successful, it will stimulate the writer emotionally. Writing is not only a form of communication; it is an affirmation. Let the reader identify with and contemplate what others have generously communicated. What others did when they wrote was what you will do when you write; that is, you will identify yourself; you will confirm, endorse, assert, approve and condone your reflections, observations, and conclusions. For the writer, it is the act of writing itself that helps heal wounds, identify personal philosophies, and leads to an understanding of his and our place in the universe. To the religious, it is a spiritual journey.

Poetry and creative writing differ from all other artistic forms. They show fresh ways of feeling and/or knowing. Someone said, "Poetry is the language in which we explore amazement." Art of any kind brings order out of chaos. It finds meaning in all aspects of life including terror, sex, beauty, war. It could be said that art undresses the world. The poet and creative writer act as a window and often speak to the reader subliminally (*limin*, Latin, 'the threshold'). Learn to recognize the symbiotic relationships between art and the life of the spirit. The act of writing creatively allows and assists us to experience perceptual and emotional growth. Jacques Maritain, the French Neo-Thomistic philosopher, stated, "I...point out the benefits men receive from poetry. Though in themselves of no help to the attainment of eternal life, art and poetry are more necessary than bread to the human race. They fit it for the life of the spirit."

"All that mankind has done, thought, gained, or been: it is lying as in magic preservation in the pages of books."

(Thomas Carlyle)

As an assignment, read a good book and understand what it was that inspired you within its pages. Then take a piece of paper and let words fall from a pen or the keyboard. Try to follow the words as you would a path in the woods. Explore with the words. Don't rationalize, forget logic. Let the words lead you to wherever they want to go.

Happy journey!

15

Summary

Creativity "is one of those hypnotic words which are prone to cast a spell upon our understanding and dissolve our thinking into haze. And out of this nebulous state of the intellect springs a strange but widely prevalent idea. The shaping spirit of the imagination sits aloof, like God...creating in some thaumaturgic fashion out of nothing its visionary world.... The ways of creation are wrapt in mystery; we may only marvel, and bow our head."

(Einstein)

In his Nobel Prize address, William Faulkner said he believed that a writer must deal with "the problems of the human heart in conflict with itself...leaving no rooom in his workshop for anything but the old verities and truths of the heart." The key to writing is honesty. Listen to your heart first, then write with your head. The mythical patterns are intrinsic to the human soul and will evolve naturally in your writing. The aesthete (one who percieves) is in each of us if we are willing to take the time to look and listen and feel. If we do, if we stop the incessant chatter of our inner voice and let the voice of the universe enter, sensitivity and imgination and intuition will take hold and the creative muse will follow.

Man's existence is defined by thought. Thought is understood via the medium of words. One of the most common forms of communication is story telling. The most revealing stories are myths. They reflect the very core of human attitudes, the inner domain of the human psyche, history, ehtics, religion, in sum, human thought combined with human language with at least a hint of the universal.

As we noted earlier, man is the only being who is conscious of being conscious and a writer is a being who can watch himself watching and write about it. Remember as a writer to take time, to notice each thing so that each thing gets noticed. A. Nin said, "We write to taste life twice."

Don't question whether to write and don't procrastinate doing it. Get on with the elation of living. Since we are never going to know the secret of life, we must take the responsibility to do what we can do, namely, witness and celebrate. Take a chance. Make a difference. There is no proof

"We have reached a crossroads in human evolution where the only road which leads forward is toward a common passion…[T]o continue to place our hopes in a social order achieved by external violence would simply amount to our giving up all hope of carrying the spirit of the Earth to its limits." These words, written by Fr. Pierre Teilhard de Chardin, come back again and again to haunt me. They were written after he had experienced the horrors of World War I. Already ordained, he nevertheless volunteered to be a stretcher bearer. Today, as I read the papers, watch the television news, and hear about similar events on the radio, it seems that for every two steps we take forward, we slip back one (sometimes visa versa!). Samuel Johnson (1709-1784) wrote: "It is the writer's duty to make the world better." To accomplish this, it is my opinion that three aspects of the human psyche need to be developed, namely: imagination, inspiration, and creativity.

I was as a gem concealed;
Me my burning ray revealed

Koran

Remember the etymology of enthusism is 'in or of God'.

"Years may wrinkle the skin, but to give up enthusiasm wrinkles the soul."

(Douglas MacArthur)

Consciousness including enthusiasm, inspiration and creativity does not come from the brain. The brain is simply an organ. It focuses and draws consciousness in and directs it but the source of consciousness is the universal consciousness of which we as individuals are only a part. We must never give up the love of wonder which lives in every human heart nor the child-like appetite, amazement and joy for everything that is new.

The creative arts are part of consciousness. The creativity aspect of that consciousness draws upon a part of our thought process that cannot be explained rationally. Passion cannot be explained rationally. Think of all the energy it takes to fight and argue as if winning were the cure. However, the passion to which I am referring is not anger. No, the passion I refer to is the result of an intoxication with life. It is the wonder and delight we feel if we just take the time to look and see, to listen and hear.

For the artist, there is a clarity and an order in the beauty of nature. Our participation in and with nature allows us to recognize that fact. The writer must allow imagination to wander and then reshape the images into something new. The more cognitive we get as a society, the further removed we become from the intuitive experience. We need myth, magic, and metaphor to stimulate our creative minds.

We must remember, we do not exist in this world isolated. We are not only social beings, we are part of the very nature which surrounds us. We shape the world and the world shapes us.

> "The secret of artistic creation and the effectiveness of art is to be found in a return to the state of 'participation mystique'—to that level of experience at which it is man who lives, and not the individual...."
>
> (Carl Jung)

Perhaps, as Carl Jung and Teilhard de Chardin and so many others have suggested, the actual fate of the world will grow out of what happens in the minds of men. Man, Rudolf Steiner states in his philosophy of education, is gifted with a soul and is here to give the spirit a dwelling place:

"I look into the world in which the sun is shining, in which the stars are sparkling, in which the stones repose...I look into the soul that lives within my being: the world-creator moves in sunlight and in soul-light, in wide world space without, in soul-depths within."

Dogwood Lane   © 2004 Ed Knepley
http://www.pbase.com/ed_k/

"Oh, beauty, ever ancient and ever new."
                              (St. Augustine)

I hope this little book has touched the creative muse lurking inside of you, tickled your fancy, and wet your appetite. It is not necessary to put the pressure of publication as a goal; far better, and more fun, to write for the sake of writing. Remember, it is the process not the product. As Phyllis Whitney says, learn to "think with a pencil". What comes out on paper may be the most wonderful gift you have ever received and, just think, you gave it to yourself!

About the Author

This book was originally written as the result of teaching/facilitating/encouraging creative writers to write. Patricia Daly-Lipe originally created the course at Maryland Hall for the Creative Arts in Annapolis and went on to teach at colleges, universities and writing centers in Maryland, Virginia, and California. Some of this text was also used as part of her doctoral dissertation.

Dr. Daly-Lipe has also combined a collection of short stories published in various magazines over the years into a book called *Nature's Wisdom*. In the year 2000, as a result of writing a series of weekly articles for La Jolla Village News celebrating the millennium, Daly-Lipe was asked to write a book bringing together those articles for Sunbelt Publications. The result, *La Jolla, A Celebration of Its Past*, won the 2002 San Diego Book Awards. In 2004, after fourteen years of research, her first historical fiction was published. *Forbidden Loves, Paris Between the Wars* takes place 1927-1939 and explores a fascinating era of innovation on all levels, from Lindbergh to James Joyce, from Picasso to Joseph Campbell, the book offers a glimpse at the glitz that was Paris while depicting aviation history in the making, the American exile community, modern art, Hannibal, the Catholic church and a moving love story.

Dr. Daly-Lipe encourages you to stay in touch. Go to: http://www.literarylady.com and check for her latest events and presentations. She may be in your area sometime soon and would love to meet you.